TensorFlow Developer Certification Guide

Crack Google's Official Exam on Getting Skilled with managing production-grade ML models

Patrick J

Published by: GitforGits
Publisher: Sonal Dhandre
www.gitforgits.com
support@gitforgits.com

Printed in India

First Printing: August 2023

ISBN: 978-8119177325

Cover Design by: Kitten Publishing

Prologue

The ability to extract useful information from large amounts of data is becoming increasingly important in this day and age, when data is being generated at a rate that has never been seen before. The ways in which we comprehend and engage with the world around us have undergone a sea change as a result of the development of artificial intelligence subfields known as machine learning and deep learning. These subfields enable computers to learn from and make predictions based on data. These technologies are reshaping industries and determining the future in a variety of areas, including healthcare, finance, entertainment, and transportation. TensorFlow is one of the tools and frameworks that are available, but it stands out as one of the most popular and powerful options available. It helps facilitate the development of machine learning models.

This book is a guide that has been painstakingly crafted with the intention of providing you with an in-depth understanding of TensorFlow and the numerous applications that it has. This is a journey that starts with the fundamentals, which involves deciphering the fundamental principles that govern machine learning, and then gradually leads you into more complex territories, during which you will investigate the complexities of neural networks, model optimization, and production deployment.

The organization of the book has been planned in such a way that it can cater to readers with varying degrees of knowledge. The first few chapters are broken down into manageable chunks that lay a strong foundation in data preprocessing, model building, and evaluation. Beginners will find these chapters to be approachable. The hands-on examples that illustrate the practical implementation of Convolutional Neural Networks (CNNs), Recurrent Neural Networks (RNNs), and other advanced techniques are sure to be appreciated by readers who are further along in their reading journey. Discover valuable insights into cutting-edge topics such as Generative Adversarial Networks (GANs), Transformer architecture, and Edge Computing with TensorFlow Lite. This book is intended for professionals with a significant amount of professional experience.

The guide places a strong emphasis on practical, real-world application, which is one of the distinguishing features of the guide. Theoretical ideas are made more clear by walking through demonstrations step by step, examining code snippets, and participating in hands-on activities. These examples are not limited to theoretical concepts but rather are based on problems that occur in the real world. As a result, you will have the opportunity to apply what you have learned to a variety of different fields.

In the latter half of the book, the author focuses on putting TensorFlow models into production, which is an important aspect that is frequently neglected in academic settings but absolutely necessary in a professional setting. The book offers in-depth guidance on how to make the transition from the development stage to the deployment stage as smooth and error-free as possible, covering topics such as serving models with TensorFlow Serving and running them in a Kubernetes cluster.

Another major focus of the book is on how to study for the TensorFlow Developer Certification exam. The guide is designed to align with the objectives of the test and includes strategies, tips, and challenges that will provide you with the knowledge as well as the confidence you need to succeed.

Last but not least, this book is more than just a technical manual; rather, it is a reflection of the ongoing evolution of Machine Learning and the transformative potential that it possesses. It is about giving people the tools they need to harness the power of data, to innovate and create, and to contribute to a future in which humanity and technology coexist harmoniously.

This book is your companion no matter where you are in your journey through the world of TensorFlow; whether you are just beginning your journey or are looking to deepen your understanding. It isn't just about picking up new information; rather, it's about feeling the thrill of discovery, the accomplishment of mastery, and the fulfillment of creation. You have arrived at the beginning of a trip that will hopefully be interesting, educational, and beneficial to you. We are excited to have you join us in the world of TensorFlow.

Content

Preface

Designed with both beginners and professionals in mind, the book is meticulously structured to cover a broad spectrum of concepts, applications, and hands-on practices that form the core of the TensorFlow Developer Certificate exam.

Starting with foundational concepts, the book guides you through the fundamental aspects of TensorFlow, Machine Learning algorithms, and Deep Learning models. The initial chapters focus on data preprocessing, exploratory analysis, and essential tools required for building robust models. The book then delves into Convolutional Neural Networks (CNNs), Long Short-Term Memory Networks (LSTMs), and advanced neural network techniques such as GANs and Transformer Architecture. Emphasizing practical application, each chapter is peppered with detailed explanations, code snippets, and real-world examples, allowing you to apply the concepts in various domains such as text classification, sentiment analysis, object detection, and more. A distinctive feature of the book is its focus on various optimization and regularization techniques that enhance model performance.

As the book progresses, it navigates through the complexities of deploying TensorFlow models into production. It includes exhaustive sections on TensorFlow Serving, Kubernetes Cluster, and edge computing with TensorFlow Lite. The book provides practical insights into monitoring, updating, and handling possible errors in production, ensuring a smooth transition from development to deployment. The final chapters are devoted to preparing you for the TensorFlow Developer Certificate exam. From strategies, tips, and coding challenges to a summary of the entire learning journey, these sections serve as a robust toolkit for exam readiness. With hints and solutions provided for challenges, you can assess your knowledge and fine-tune your problem-solving skills.

The book provides:

- Comprehensive guide to TensorFlow, covering fundamentals to advanced topics, aiding seamless learning.
- Alignment with TensorFlow Developer Certificate exam, providing targeted preparation and confidence.
- In-depth exploration of neural networks, enhancing understanding of model architecture and function.
- Hands-on examples throughout, ensuring practical understanding and immediate applicability of concepts.
- Detailed insights into model optimization, including regularization, boosting model performance.
- Extensive focus on deployment, from TensorFlow Serving to Kubernetes, for real-world applications.

- Exploration of innovative technologies like BiLSTM, attention mechanisms, Transformers, fostering creativity.
- Step-by-step coding challenges, enhancing problem-solving skills, mirroring real-world scenarios.
- Coverage of potential errors in deployment, offering practical solutions, ensuring robust applications.
- Continual emphasis on practical, applicable knowledge, making it suitable for all levels.

In essence, this book is more than a mere certification guide; it's a complete roadmap to mastering TensorFlow. It aligns perfectly with the objectives of the TensorFlow Developer Certificate exam, ensuring that you are not only well-versed in the theoretical aspects but are also skilled in practical applications.

GitforGits

Prerequisites

Whether you're an aspiring data scientist, a seasoned professional, or someone curious about the world of TensorFlow, this book is your gateway to success in building TensorFlow-based Machine Learning systems and get certified by official TensorFlow certification.

Codes Usage

Are you in need of some helpful code examples to assist you in your programming and documentation? Look no further! Our book offers a wealth of supplemental material, including code examples and exercises.

Not only is this book here to aid you in getting your job done, but you have our permission to use the example code in your programs and documentation. However, please note that if you are reproducing a significant portion of the code, we do require you to contact us for permission.

But don't worry, using several chunks of code from this book in your program or answering a question by citing our book and quoting example code does not require permission. But if you do choose to give credit, an attribution typically includes the title, author, publisher, and ISBN. For example, "TensorFlow Developer Certification Guide by Patrick J".

If you are unsure whether your intended use of the code examples falls under fair use or the permissions outlined above, please do not hesitate to reach out to us at support@gitforgits.com.

We are happy to assist and clarify any concerns.

Acknowledgement

I owe a tremendous debt of gratitude to GitforGits, for their unflagging enthusiasm and wise counsel throughout the entire process of writing this book. Their knowledge and careful editing helped make sure the piece was useful for people of all reading levels and comprehension skills. In addition, I'd like to thank everyone involved in the publishing process for their efforts in making this book a reality. Their efforts, from copyediting to advertising, made the project what it is today.

Finally, I'd like to express my gratitude to everyone who has shown me unconditional love and encouragement throughout my life. Their support was crucial to the completion of this book. I appreciate your help with this endeavour and your continued interest in my career.

CHAPTER 1: INTRODUCTION TO MACHINE LEARNING AND TENSORFLOW 2.X

Machine Learning: A Brief History

Machine learning's origins can be traced back to the early 20th century with the development of mathematical theories that would later become essential in machine learning. In the 1900s, regression analysis was formalized, laying the foundation for predictive modeling. Mathematical statistics also emerged as a discipline, introducing key concepts like hypothesis testing and confidence intervals.

In the 1930s and 40s, linear discriminant analysis was invented for pattern classification tasks. Around the same time, the first neural network model was proposed, inspired by the biological neural networks in brains. In the 1950s, Alan Turing's pioneering work on the Turing Test sparked significant interest in artificial intelligence and machine learning. Turing proposed that if a machine could exhibit behavior indistinguishable from a human, we may consider it "intelligent".

The Advent of Neural Networks

The late 1950s marked a major milestone with the invention of the Perceptron by Frank Rosenblatt. The Perceptron algorithm enabled machines to automatically learn and improve from data. This sparked enthusiasm about the potential for AI and learning machines. However, the limitations of early algorithms like Perceptrons soon became apparent. For example, Perceptrons struggled with the XOR problem, unable to learn non-linearly separable functions.

The AI Winter

The initial hype around machine learning led to inflated expectations that could not be immediately realized with the constraints of contemporary hardware and algorithms. When early AI systems failed to live up to the hype, research funding dried up, beginning the first "AI winter" in the 1970s. Progress slowed as interest and optimism in AI and machine learning waned.

The Revival of Neural Networks

The second AI winter arrived in the late 1980s and early 90s. While neural networks showed promise, research was impeded by the difficulty in training deeper multi-layer networks. The computational power required to train neural nets with multiple hidden layers was prohibitive at the time. The resurgence of neural networks began in the 1990s with the development of backpropagation. This algorithm enabled the iterative adjustment of weights in multilayer networks, revitalizing research in deep learning. With backpropagation, networks with multiple hidden layers could be effectively trained.

The Era of Big Data

In the 1990s and 2000s, new algorithms broadened the application domains for machine learning. Support Vector Machines (SVMs) improved performance on pattern recognition tasks. Random decision forests introduced an ensemble method combining multiple decision trees to create more robust models. The exponential growth of data and increase in affordable computing power provided the foundation for the success of modern machine learning. The emergence of big data from social media, e-commerce, science, and other fields provided vast datasets to train machine learning models. The development of graphics processing units (GPUs) accelerated training of neural networks.

Deep Learning and Modern Success

Deep learning breakthroughs built upon this data and computing foundation, leading to superhuman performance on complex tasks. In 2012, a deep convolutional neural network called AlexNet by Hinton, Krizhevsky and others decimated the competition in the ImageNet object recognition challenge, igniting widespread interest in deep learning.

Natural language processing experienced major advances with models like bidirectional long short-term memory (LSTM) networks, Transformer-based models such as BERT and GPT-3, and attention mechanisms. Computer vision continued to progress with object detection models like YOLO and Faster R-CNN for real-time processing.

Reinforcement learning combined with neural networks led to superhuman gameplay in Go, chess, Atari games and more. Generative adversarial networks (GANs) produced remarkably realistic synthetic images, video, and audio. The success across application areas firmly established deep learning as a foundational tool for machine learning practitioners.

Future Aspects

While the history of machine learning has seen ups and downs, the field continues to evolve rapidly, adapting to new opportunities and challenges. Ethical implications of machine learning systems are coming under scrutiny, highlighting the need for fairness, interpretability, and transparency in AI. As models become more advanced, maintaining security and control also becomes critical.

Emerging directions for machine learning research include ways to reduce reliance on huge datasets, combining neural networks with symbolic logic and knowledge representations, integration of neuroscience insights, and advances in natural language interfaces. Quantum machine learning offers potential speedups by applying quantum computing to machine learning algorithms. Machine learning deployment in real-world contexts will require responding to shifting landscapes of data availability, privacy regulations, systemic biases, and the threat of misuse by malicious actors. Maintaining public trust and shaping policy frameworks to ensure democratization of machine learning benefits will be pivotal.

As machine learning continues permeating various spheres of life, from personalized medicine and education to smart cities and autonomous transportation, multidisciplinary collaboration and open communication channels between technologists, domain experts, businesses, policymakers, and the general public will be key. With responsible development, machine learning promises innovative solutions to improve human lives.

Deep Learning Fundamentals

Deep learning is a specialized branch of machine learning, distinguished by its use of algorithms that draw inspiration from the structural and functional intricacies of the human brain. These computational algorithms are commonly referred to as artificial neural networks. Unlike traditional machine learning techniques, deep learning dives much deeper into data analysis, hence the name "deep learning." The models in this category have multiple layers of interconnected nodes that work together to analyze various aspects of the data. These multi-layered networks can digest, interpret, and make sense of large sets of data, ranging from text to images and sound, and everything in between. They excel at identifying intricate patterns, structures, and variations in the data, which would be incomprehensible or highly challenging for a human or less complex algorithms. One of the most attractive features of deep learning is its capability to operate autonomously, meaning it can make data-driven decisions without requiring human intervention.

Deep learning models are particularly potent when dealing with 'big data.' They are designed to automatically and adaptively learn from this massive influx of information, adjusting their algorithms accordingly to improve their performance. Because of this, they are incredibly effective for tasks like image and speech recognition, natural language processing, and even game-playing, among many other applications. These models are self-adjusting, refining their internal parameters based on the feedback they receive from the performance of their predictions. This allows them to continuously improve, making them highly reliable for a variety of complex tasks that are pivotal in today's technologically driven world. They are often employed in critical sectors like healthcare for disease diagnosis, in automotive industries for self-driving cars, and in customer service as chatbots. Overall, deep learning offers a transformative approach to machine learning, promising innovative solutions across various industries.

Artificial Neural Networks (ANNs)

Artificial neural networks (ANNs) are inspired by biological neural networks and how neurons in the brain process information. At the core of an ANN are artificial neurons that receive inputs, perform computations, and pass data on to other neurons.

ANNs consist of layers of interconnected artificial neurons:

- Input Layer: The input layer receives the raw data that is fed into the network. This layer passes the data on to the next layer in the network.
- Hidden Layers: ANNs contain one or more hidden layers between the input and output layers. Hidden layers apply transformations to the data by processing the weighted input

signals from the previous layer. Multiple hidden layers allow deep neural networks to learn highly complex relationships and features in the data.

- Output Layer: The output layer produces the prediction or classification result based on the inputs propagated through the network. The output could be a categorical classification, numerical value regression, or multidimensional tensor output.

Neurons and Activation Functions

At the level of individual neurons, several steps occur:

- Weighted Inputs: Each input to the neuron is multiplied by a weight value. These weights determine how much influence the respective inputs have on the neuron's output.
- Bias: A bias value is added to the weighted inputs as an additional trainable parameter. The bias shifts the activation function and controls when a neuron fires.
- Activation Function: The weighted sum plus bias is fed into the neuron's activation function, which converts the input signals to an output signal. The activation function introduces non-linearity into the network.

Common activation functions include:

- ReLU (Rectified Linear Unit). Returns the maximum of zero or the input value, enabling faster training.
- Sigmoid: Squashes values between 0 and 1, useful for binary classification problems.
- Tanh (Hyperbolic Tangent): Maps values between -1 and 1, providing zero centered outputs.

The interconnection of artificial neurons stacked into multiple layers gives ANNs the ability to extract complex features, relationships, and patterns from raw data. Through techniques like backpropagation, the weights and biases across the network layers are iteratively updated during training to minimize the model's loss. This tuning of millions of parameters is what allows deep neural networks to achieve remarkable performance on tasks like image recognition, language translation, and prediction.

How Learning Happens?

Forward and Backward Pass

The learning process in deep neural networks relies on forward and backward passes:

- Forward Pass: During the forward pass, data is fed through the network from the input layer to the output layer. Each neuron receives inputs from the previous layer, calculates a weighted sum with biases, applies its activation function, and passes its output to neurons in the next layer. Ultimately, a prediction is generated at the output layer.
- Backward Pass (Backpropagation): The network's weights and biases are updated through backpropagation. First, a loss function compares the prediction to the true target value

and calculates the error. Then, through the backpropagation algorithm, the gradient of the loss with respect to each weight and bias is calculated. Finally, the optimizer updates the weights and biases to reduce the loss.

Several key components come into play:

Loss Functions

A loss function measures how well the network's predictions match the actual values. Common loss functions include:

- Mean Squared Error (MSE): Used for regression problems.
- Cross-Entropy Loss: Used for classification problems.

Optimizers

Optimizers adjust the weights and biases in the network to minimize the loss. Popular optimizers include:

- Gradient Descent: Adjusts the weights and biases in the direction that reduces the loss.
- Stochastic Gradient Descent (SGD): Uses a subset of data at each step, making learning faster.
- Adam: A more advanced optimizer that adapts the learning rate during training.

Overfitting and Regularization

Overfitting occurs when a model learns the training data too well, including its noise and outliers, and performs poorly on new data. Regularization techniques prevent overfitting by adding constraints to the learning process. Common techniques include dropout, where random neurons are "turned off" during training, and L1/L2 regularization, where penalties are added to the loss function.

Deep Learning Models

Different deep learning models are used for various tasks:

- Convolutional Neural Networks (CNNs): Specialized for image data, using filters to detect patterns such as edges, textures, and shapes.
- Recurrent Neural Networks (RNNs): Designed for sequential data like time series or natural language, where the order of the data matters.
- Generative Adversarial Networks (GANs): Comprise two networks that compete, one to generate data, the other to discriminate between real and generated data.

These fundamental concepts are the building blocks of deep learning, and they range from a comprehension of the fundamentals of neurons and layers to an understanding of how learning occurs through forward and backward passes. These foundations prepare us for our exploration of TensorFlow, where you will see how these principles are put into practise to build, train, and deploy deep learning models. You will do this by examining activation functions, loss functions, optimizers, and specific models such as CNNs and RNNs.

Introduction to TensorFlow 2.x

Google is the company that created the open-source machine learning library known as TensorFlow. It is intended to assist developers and researchers in the construction and deployment of machine learning models, and more specifically deep learning models. The name TensorFlow comes from the multi-dimensional arrays, also known as tensors, that the software is able to handle. This software makes it possible for data to flow through a flow graph or a series of mathematical operations.

Let us investigate its most important characteristics and capabilities:

Flexibility and Ease of Use

- High-level APIs: TensorFlow offers high-level APIs like Keras, simplifying model creation, training, and deployment.
- Eager Execution: Enables immediate evaluation of operations, facilitating a more interactive front-end to TensorFlow and making debugging more intuitive.
- Comprehensive Libraries: Comes with numerous libraries and extensions for tasks ranging from image analysis to quantum computing.

Performance Optimization

- GPU and TPU Support: TensorFlow can run on multiple GPUs and TPUs, offering high performance for training and inference.
- Graph Optimization: TensorFlow automatically translates the defined model into an optimized series of computations to improve efficiency.
- Mixed Precision Training: Utilizes both 16-bit and 32-bit floating-point types to make model training faster and require less memory.

Scalability

- Distributed Training: Supports distributed training across various hardware setups, accommodating large-scale models and datasets.
- Multi-platform Compatibility: Works on different platforms including mobile, embedded, and browser environments, allowing for a wide range of applications.

Extensive Model Support

- Pre-trained Models: Offers a collection of pre-trained models, reducing development time.
- Custom Model Building: Provides tools to build custom architectures tailored for specific

problems.

- Support for Various Neural Networks: Whether it's CNNs for image processing, RNNs for sequence data, or GANs for generative tasks, TensorFlow provides the necessary tools.

Robust Data Handling

- TensorFlow Data (tf.data): An API designed for building complex input pipelines from simple and reusable pieces, managing large datasets efficiently.
- Data Augmentation: Tools to transform and augment data, enhancing the training process.

Visualization and Debugging

- TensorBoard: A suite of visualization tools making the training process transparent and debuggable.
- Model Evaluation Tools: Assists in understanding how well models are performing through various metrics and visualizations.

Production Readiness

- TensorFlow Serving: A flexible and high-performance serving system for deploying machine learning models.
- TensorFlow Lite: Enables deployment of models on mobile and IoT devices with low latency.
- TensorFlow.js: Brings machine learning to JavaScript, allowing model training and inference directly in the browser or on Node.js.

TensorFlow is not just a tool but an extensive ecosystem that accommodates various needs across research, development, and production in the machine learning domain. Its flexibility, performance optimization, scalability, and strong community support make it appealing for beginners and experts alike. By exploring its capabilities, one gains the necessary foundation to dive into building, training, and deploying diverse machine learning models. Whether it's understanding complex data patterns, creating next-generation applications, or pushing the boundaries of academic research, TensorFlow serves as an essential platform in the modern machine learning landscape. It's the bridge between learning the theoretical fundamentals of deep learning and applying them in the real world, aligning perfectly with the objective of passing the TensorFlow Developer Certificate Exam.

TensorFlow 2.x Installation: Using pip

It is a simple process to install TensorFlow on a Linux operating system by using pip, which is Python's package installer. You will be well-prepared to begin working with TensorFlow on your Linux machine if you follow the steps that are outlined below.

Check Python Version

TensorFlow requires Python 3.6 & above. Make sure you have the compatible version installed:

```
python3 --version
```

If you need to install or upgrade Python, follow the instructions specific to your Linux distribution.

Install pip

Ensure that you have the latest version of pip. You can install or upgrade pip by running:

```
sudo apt update
sudo apt install python3-pip
```

Create Virtual Environment

Creating a virtual environment allows you to isolate TensorFlow from other Python packages, minimizing potential conflicts. You can create a virtual environment using the following commands:

```
python3 -m venv myenv
source myenv/bin/activate
```

Replace "myenv" with your desired environment name. To deactivate the environment, just type deactivate.

Choose TensorFlow Version

TensorFlow comes in different flavors:

- TensorFlow with CPU support only: Suitable for machine learning development and computational tasks that don't require significant GPU acceleration.
- TensorFlow with GPU support: If you have a compatible Nvidia GPU, you can install

TensorFlow with GPU support to benefit from hardware acceleration.

Install TensorFlow with CPU Support

To install TensorFlow compatible with your CPU, make sure you are inside your virtual environment, and run:

```
pip install tensorflow
```

This will install the latest stable version of TensorFlow with CPU support.

Install TensorFlow with GPU Support

If you have a compatible GPU and want to utilize it with TensorFlow, follow these steps:

Install CUDA and cuDNN

TensorFlow with GPU support requires specific versions of NVIDIA's CUDA and cuDNN libraries. Refer to NVIDIA's official tutorial to install these.

Install GPU-supported TensorFlow

Within your virtual environment, run:

```
pip install tensorflow-gpu
```

This installs TensorFlow with GPU support.

Verify TensorFlow Installation

You can verify your installation by starting a Python interpreter and running:

```
import tensorflow as tf
print(tf.__version__)
```

This will print the installed version of TensorFlow, confirming a successful installation.

System-Specific Adjustments

While these steps provide a baseline TensorFlow installation on Linux, further customization may be required. Some Linux distributions could necessitate installing extra system libraries like CUDA or cuDNN for GPU acceleration. Configuring GPUs for hardware acceleration, managing virtual environments, and resolving driver compatibility issues represent additional configuration tasks. Nonetheless, these above steps set up a fundamental TensorFlow environment to start building and training machine learning models on Linux, opening the door to research, development, and experimentation.

Tensors

Tensors are the primary focus of TensorFlow's collection of data structures. They are generalizations of vectors and matrices to higher dimensions and come in the form of multidimensional arrays. Tensors are used to transport numeric data through the various machine learning operations as they move between nodes in computational graphs. Understanding tensors is essential if you want to make the most of TensorFlow's capabilities.

Tensors have characteristics such as rank and shape, in addition to data types. The number of dimensions is referred to as the rank, the size along each axis is described by the shape, and the data type is the representation of the numeric data itself, such as 32-bit floats or 64-bit integers.

Tensors allow us to express a wide variety of computations in a unified format. Tensors allow for the indexing, slicing, and reshaping of data in various ways. Vectorized arithmetic is accomplished through the use of element-wise operations such as addition and multiplication, concatenation, reductions, and broadcasting. Multiplication of tensors, slicing and joining patches, applying custom functions, and other more complex operations are examples of more advanced operations.

TensorFlow is centered, fundamentally, on the concept of composable tensor operations. Tensors are useful for representing and transforming numeric data because they offer a generalized n-dimensional array structure. The capabilities of the TensorFlow framework for machine learning, scientific computing, and other fields will be unlocked once we have mastered the idiomatic manipulation of tensors in that framework. Because of its adaptable architecture, TensorFlow gives us the ability to construct and deploy highly specialized computational graphs.

Creating Tensors in TensorFlow

You can create tensors using various TensorFlow functions. The given below are some examples:

```
import tensorflow as tf

# Scalar (0D tensor)
scalar_tensor = tf.constant(5)
```

```
# Vector (1D tensor)
vector_tensor = tf.constant([1, 2, 3])

# Matrix (2D tensor)
matrix_tensor = tf.constant([[1, 2], [3, 4]])

# Higher-dimensional tensor
higher_dimension_tensor = tf.constant([[[1, 2], [3, 4]], [[5, 6], [7, 8]]])
```

Perform Tensor Operations

Element-wise Operations

You can perform standard arithmetic operations on tensors, such as addition, subtraction, multiplication, and division.

```
a = tf.constant([1, 2, 3])
b = tf.constant([4, 5, 6])

addition = tf.add(a, b)
subtraction = tf.subtract(a, b)
multiplication = tf.multiply(a, b)
division = tf.divide(a, b)
```

Matrix Multiplication

You can multiply matrices using tf.matmul.

```
mat1 = tf.constant([[1, 2], [3, 4]])
mat2 = tf.constant([[5, 6], [7, 8]])

result = tf.matmul(mat1, mat2)
```

Reshaping

You can reshape tensors using tf.reshape.

```
tensor = tf.constant([[1, 2, 3], [4, 5, 6]])
reshaped_tensor = tf.reshape(tensor, (3, 2))
```

Casting

You can change the data type of a tensor using tf.cast.

```
tensor = tf.constant([1.0, 2.0, 3.0])
tensor_int = tf.cast(tensor, tf.int32)
```

Aggregation

You can perform aggregations like sum, mean, and maximum.

```
tensor = tf.constant([1, 2, 3])

sum_tensor = tf.reduce_sum(tensor)
mean_tensor = tf.reduce_mean(tensor)
max_tensor = tf.reduce_max(tensor)
```

Slicing and Indexing

You can access specific parts of a tensor using standard indexing and slicing.

```
tensor = tf.constant([[1, 2, 3], [4, 5, 6]])
first_row = tensor[0]
first_element = tensor[0, 0]
```

Broadcasting

TensorFlow allows for broadcasting, where you can perform operations between tensors of different shapes, and TensorFlow will automatically expand the dimensions as needed.

```
a = tf.constant([1, 2, 3])
b = tf.constant(2)
broadcasted_multiplication = a * b # Equivalent to [2, 4, 6]
```

Through the above illustrated samples around creating and manipulating tensors using the above operations, you can gain hands-on experience and a solid understanding of how tensors function within TensorFlow. Whether for data preprocessing, model construction, or result interpretation, tensors and their operations are integral to the journey from novice to expert TensorFlow developer.

Advanced Tensor Operations

Strengthening your understanding of tensor operations involves diving deeper into more advanced functionalities and exploring various use-cases. Let us continue by looking at some more sophisticated tensor operations that are commonly used in practice.

Transposing Tensors

Transposing a tensor involves swapping its axes, and it's a common operation especially in linear algebra.

```
tensor = tf.constant([[1, 2], [3, 4]])
transposed_tensor = tf.transpose(tensor)
```

Tensor Sorting and Argsort

Sorting a tensor or getting the indices that would sort it is useful for ranking elements.

```
tensor = tf.constant([5, 2, 3, 1])
sorted_tensor = tf.sort(tensor)
sorted_indices = tf.argsort(tensor)
```

Tensor Concatenation

You can combine tensors along a specific axis using tf.concat.

```
tensor1 = tf.constant([[1, 2], [3, 4]])
tensor2 = tf.constant([[5, 6]])
concatenated_tensor = tf.concat([tensor1, tensor2], axis=0)
```

Tensor Stacking

Stacking tensors along a new axis is achieved with tf.stack.

```
tensor1 = tf.constant([1, 2])
tensor2 = tf.constant([3, 4])
stacked_tensor = tf.stack([tensor1, tensor2])
```

Tensor Splitting

You can split a tensor into sub-tensors using tf.split.

```
tensor = tf.constant([[1, 2, 3], [4, 5, 6]])
split_tensors = tf.split(tensor, num_or_size_splits=2, axis=1)
```

One-Hot Encoding

One-hot encoding transforms integer labels into binary vectors. It's essential for categorical data handling.

```
tensor = tf.constant([0, 1, 2])
one_hot_tensor = tf.one_hot(tensor, depth=3)
```

Tensor Padding

Padding adds extra zeros or other values around the tensor, commonly used in image and sequence processing.

```
tensor = tf.constant([[1, 2], [3, 4]])
padded_tensor = tf.pad(tensor, paddings=[[1, 1], [1, 1]])
```

Gather and Scatter

Gathering extracts values from a tensor using index arrays, and scatter updates a tensor using index and update arrays.

```
tensor = tf.constant([10, 20, 30, 40])
indices = [1, 3]
gathered_tensor = tf.gather(tensor, indices)
```

```
updates = [100, 200]
scatter_tensor = tf.tensor_scatter_nd_update(tensor, tf.reshape(indices, [2, 1]), updates)
```

Tensor Reduction

Reduction operations reduce tensors along specified axes, like tf.reduce_prod for products or tf.reduce_any for logical OR.

```
tensor = tf.constant([[1, 2], [3, 4]])
product_tensor = tf.reduce_prod(tensor, axis=1)
any_tensor = tf.reduce_any(tensor > 2)
```

Custom Operations with tf.function

You can define custom operations using TensorFlow's functions and automatic differentiation features.

```
@tf.function
def custom_operation(tensor):
    return tensor * 2 + 1

tensor = tf.constant([1, 2, 3])
result = custom_operation(tensor)
```

These advanced operations open up new possibilities for data manipulation and model building. Experimenting with these operations, creating small projects, and integrating them into real-world applications will strengthen your practical learning of tensor operations in TensorFlow.

Summary

In this chapter, we delved into the foundational understanding of tensors in TensorFlow and how to perform various tensor operations. Tensors, being the primary data structure in TensorFlow, are multi-dimensional arrays that enable the representation of data in various forms, from scalars to high-dimensional arrays. We explored how to create tensors, their essential attributes, and elementary operations like addition, subtraction, multiplication, and division. This set the stage for understanding the manipulation of data within TensorFlow, allowing you to visualize how basic mathematical concepts translate into computational operations.

Moving further, we introduced more advanced tensor operations such as transposing, sorting, concatenation, stacking, splitting, one-hot encoding, padding, gathering, scattering, reduction, and even custom operations. These advanced functionalities showcased the flexibility and power of TensorFlow in handling complex data manipulation tasks. From reshaping data to preparing it for specific algorithms, these operations provide the tools needed to pre-process and transform data effectively.

In addition to theoretical concepts, we emphasized hands-on examples and code snippets, enabling practical exploration of tensor operations. Through this approach, you were guided through the implementation of tensor operations, gaining valuable insights into how to apply these techniques in real-world scenarios. Practical exploration fosters a deeper understanding, transforming abstract concepts into tangible skills.

This comprehensive journey through tensors and their operations within TensorFlow equips you with the knowledge and skills required to handle data manipulation tasks in machine learning and deep learning projects. By understanding and mastering tensor operations, you are well-positioned to embark on building complex models and applications, laying a robust foundation for further exploration and innovation in the field of TensorFlow and deep learning. The skills acquired in this chapter are vital stepping stones towards becoming proficient TensorFlow developers, enabling you to manipulate data efficiently and creatively to meet various computational needs.

Chapter 2: Up and Running with Neural Networks

Introduction to Neural Networks

Neural networks serve as the foundational structure for deep learning methodologies. They mimic the intricate workings of the human brain, allowing for the identification of intricate patterns and facilitating informed decision-making processes. Gaining a thorough understanding of the various elements that constitute a neural network is crucial for anyone looking to construct and train sophisticated models tailored for a wide range of applications.

Neural networks are computational models that have revolutionized various fields, from natural language processing and computer vision to healthcare and finance. Understanding the architecture and components of neural networks is essential for anyone aiming to harness their power for complex problem-solving.

Layers and Neurons

A neural network is composed of layers, each containing a set of neurons or nodes. These layers are categorized into three main types:

- Input Layer: The initial layer that receives the raw data. Each neuron in this layer corresponds to one feature of the dataset.
- Hidden Layers: These are the layers between the input and output layers. The number of hidden layers and neurons within them can vary, affecting the network's ability to model complex relationships.
- Output Layer: The final layer produces the prediction or classification. The number of neurons here usually corresponds to the number of classes in a classification problem or a single neuron for regression tasks.

Each neuron receives input from neurons in the previous layer, applies a weighted sum along with a bias term, and then uses an activation function to produce an output. The output is then passed to neurons in the next layer.

Activation Functions

Activation functions serve as the gatekeepers of neural networks, introducing essential non-linearity into the system. This nonlinearity allows neural networks to capture complex relationships in the data, making them capable of learning from errors and fine-tuning their performance.

The most commonly used activation functions are:

- ReLU (Rectified Linear Unit): ReLU is widely used in hidden layers due to its computational efficiency. It outputs zero for negative inputs and retains positive inputs, making it ideal for many tasks.

- Sigmoid: The Sigmoid function squashes values between 0 and 1, making it useful for binary classification problems. However, it suffers from the vanishing gradient problem, which can slow down the training process.

- Tanh (Hyperbolic Tangent): Similar to Sigmoid but with a range from -1 to 1, Tanh is more balanced but still susceptible to the vanishing gradient problem.

- Softmax: Often used in the output layer for multi-class classification, Softmax converts raw scores into probabilities.

- Leaky ReLU and Parametric ReLU: Variants of ReLU that allow small, non-zero outputs for negative inputs, mitigating the "dying ReLU" problem.

Activation functions are pivotal in determining the output of a neural network and influence how quickly a network can learn and how complex functions it can approximate.

Weights and Biases

Weights and biases are the adjustable parameters that the neural network learns during the training phase. They play a critical role in the network's performance:

- Weights: These are the coefficients that control the strength and direction of the connection between neurons. They are initialized randomly and get updated during training to minimize the loss function.

- Biases: Biases are added to the weighted sum before the activation function is applied. They provide each neuron with the flexibility to activate even when the weighted sum of its inputs is not sufficient.

- Parameter Initialization: The initial values of weights and biases can significantly impact the network's performance. Methods like Xavier and He initialization are often used to set these initial values.

- Parameter Sharing: In convolutional neural networks (CNNs), the concept of parameter sharing reduces the number of trainable parameters, making the network more efficient.

Understanding the role of weights and biases, and how they are updated, is crucial for effectively training a neural network.

Forward Propagation

Forward propagation is the initial phase where the input data traverses through the network, layer by layer, until it reaches the output layer to produce a prediction. During this process:

- Weighted Sum: Each neuron calculates the weighted sum of its inputs and adds a bias term.
- Activation: The activation function is applied to this sum to produce the neuron's output.
- Data Flow: The outputs from one layer serve as inputs to the neurons in the subsequent layer.
- Prediction: The final output is generated, which could be a class label in classification tasks or a continuous value in regression tasks.

Forward propagation is the first half of the learning cycle, setting the stage for backpropagation.

Backpropagation and Gradient Descent

Backpropagation is the cornerstone of neural network training. It is the mechanism by which the network learns from its mistakes and updates its weights and biases. This process is facilitated by the optimization algorithm known as gradient descent:

- Error Calculation: The first step is to compute the error or loss by comparing the predicted output to the actual target values.
- Gradient Computation: The gradient of the loss function with respect to each weight and bias is calculated. This gradient indicates the direction and magnitude of change required to minimize the error.
- Weight and Bias Update: Using the computed gradients, the weights and biases are updated in the direction that minimizes the loss function.
- Learning Rate: This is a hyperparameter that controls the step size during the weight update. Fine-tuning the learning rate is essential for efficient training.
- Optimization Algorithms: Variants of gradient descent, like Stochastic Gradient Descent (SGD), Adam, and RMSprop, offer different ways to update the weights and biases, each with its own advantages and disadvantages.

Backpropagation and gradient descent form the crux of neural network training, enabling the model to learn complex mappings from inputs to outputs effectively.

Loss Functions

Loss functions serve as the evaluative metrics that quantify the performance of a neural network model. They act as the guiding light for the optimization algorithms, helping them understand how well the model is doing. The choice of the loss function can significantly impact the effectiveness of the training process.

- Mean Squared Error (MSE): Primarily used in regression problems, MSE measures the average of the squares of the errors between the predicted and actual values. It is sensitive to outliers and gives more weight to larger errors.

- Cross-Entropy: This is the go-to loss function for classification problems. It measures the dissimilarity between the predicted probability distribution and the actual distribution of the target classes. Lower cross-entropy indicates better model performance.

- Huber Loss: A combination of MSE and Mean Absolute Error, Huber Loss is less sensitive to outliers compared to MSE. It's often used in robust regression.

- Hinge Loss: Used for "maximum-margin" classification, primarily in Support Vector Machines.

- Log Loss: Used in logistic regression models, it measures the performance of a classification model where the prediction is a probability value between 0 and 1.

Learning Rate

The learning rate is a hyperparameter that governs the extent to which the model updates its weights during each iteration of training. It's a crucial factor that can either make or break the model's performance.

- High Learning Rate: A high learning rate can cause the model to converge rapidly, but there's a risk of overshooting the global minimum of the loss function. This could lead to unstable training and poor generalization.

- Low Learning Rate: While a low learning rate ensures more reliable convergence, it makes the training process exceedingly slow, requiring more computational resources and time.

- Adaptive Learning Rate: Methods like Adagrad, Adadelta, and Adam adjust the learning rate during training, aiming to combine the best of both worlds.

Regularization Techniques

Regularization techniques are employed to constrain the complexity of the model, thereby preventing overfitting, which occurs when the model performs well on the training data but poorly on unseen data.

- L1 Regularization: Adds the sum of the absolute values of the weights as a penalty term to the loss function. It can result in a sparse weight matrix.
- L2 Regularization: Adds the sum of the squares of the weights as a penalty term. It's more common than L1 and tends to produce small weights but not necessarily zero.
- Elastic Net: A combination of L1 and L2 regularization, it aims to minimize the limitations of both methods.
- Dropout: During training, random neurons are "dropped out" or deactivated, which helps the model to become more robust.

Batch Size and Epochs

Batch size and epochs are other critical hyperparameters that influence the training dynamics.

- Batch Size: The batch size dictates the number of samples that will be used in each iteration for updating the weights. Smaller batches often provide a regularizing effect and lower generalization error.
- Epochs: An epoch is a complete forward and backward pass of all the training samples. The model is usually trained for multiple epochs. The number of epochs is essentially the number of times the learning algorithm will cycle through the entire training dataset.
- Mini-batch and Stochastic Gradient Descent: When the batch size is less than the total dataset size, it's called mini-batch gradient descent. If the batch size is 1, it's known as stochastic gradient descent.
- Early Stopping: This technique monitors the model's performance on a validation set and stops the training process when the performance starts degrading, helping to find the optimal number of epochs.

Optimizers

Optimizers play a pivotal role in the training of neural networks by fine-tuning the model's parameters, such as weights and learning rates, to minimize the loss function. They are essentially the algorithms that guide the network in the most efficient path through the complex landscape of possible parameter values. Among the most commonly used optimizers are Adam, RMSprop, and SGD (Stochastic Gradient Descent).

- Adam (Adaptive Moment Estimation): This optimizer combines the advantages of both AdaGrad and RMSprop. It adjusts the learning rate for each parameter, providing benefits of both methods. It's often recommended for problems that are large in terms of data and parameters.

- RMSprop (Root Mean Square Propagation): This optimizer adjusts the learning rate during training. It uses a moving average of squared gradients to normalize the gradient itself, which means it adapts the learning rates during training.

- SGD (Stochastic Gradient Descent): The most traditional form of optimization algorithm, it updates each parameter with respect to the gradient of the error with respect to that parameter, provided the value of the learning rate.

Understanding the nuances of these optimizers can significantly impact the efficiency and effectiveness of the neural network training process.

Initialization Methods

The initial values of the weights in a neural network can significantly influence the training dynamics. Proper weight initialization can lead to faster convergence and lower training error. Two of the most popular methods for weight initialization are Xavier and He initialization.

- Xavier Initialization: Also known as Glorot Initialization, this method sets the initial weights in such a way that the variance remains the same for both inputs and outputs. This is particularly useful for Sigmoid activation functions or hyperbolic tangent activation functions.

- He Initialization: Named after Kaiming He, this method is designed specifically for ReLU (Rectified Linear Units) activation functions. It initializes the weights in a way that mitigates the problem of vanishing gradients in deep networks.

Selecting the appropriate initialization method can accelerate the training process and improve the model's performance, especially in deep neural networks.

Dropout and Batch Normalization

- Dropout: Dropout is a regularization technique aimed at reducing overfitting in neural networks. During the training phase, random neurons are "dropped out" or temporarily deactivated, meaning they do not participate in the forward or backward pass. This forces the network to learn more robust features that are useful in conjunction with many different random subsets of the other neurons.

- Batch Normalization: This technique aims to improve the training of deep neural networks. It normalizes the output from the activation function of neurons within a layer for each mini-batch. This means that during training, each neuron's output will have a mean close to 0 and a standard deviation close to 1. This normalization helps to combat the internal covariate shift problem, where the distribution of each layer's inputs changes during training, slowing down the training process and making it harder to train models with non-linear activation functions.

Both Dropout and Batch Normalization are essential techniques for improving the generalization capability of neural networks and making them more robust to the variations in the training data.

To summarize, neural networks are complex models composed of layers, neurons, activation functions, and various techniques to train and evaluate them. Understanding each of these components and how they interact will equip you with the knowledge to build, train, and implement neural networks effectively for a multitude of tasks further in this chapter.

Sample Program: Linear Regression using Neural Network

Building upon our previous discussion of neural networks in the previous section, let us delve into a real-world application by executing simple linear regression through a neural network framework. Simple linear regression serves as a statistical technique that aims to establish a linear relationship between a target variable and a single predictor variable by fitting them to a linear equation. In the given below example, you will concentrate on employing simple linear regression involving just one predictor variable.

Problem Definition

Suppose we want to predict the price of houses based on their square footage. You will use a neural network with a single neuron to model this relationship.

Dataset Preparation

First, we need a dataset containing square footage and corresponding house prices.

```
import numpy as np

# Example data
square_footage = np.array([1000, 1500, 2000, 2500, 3000])
house_prices = np.array([100000, 150000, 200000, 250000, 300000])
```

Creating the Neural Network

You will create a neural network with one neuron, one input, and one output.

```
import tensorflow as tf

# Model architecture
model = tf.keras.Sequential([
    tf.keras.layers.Dense(1, input_shape=[1])
])
```

Compiling the Model

We need to define the loss function and the optimizer. Since it's a regression problem, Mean Squared Error (MSE) is a suitable loss function, and you will use Adam optimizer.

```
model.compile(optimizer='adam', loss='mse')
```

Training the Model

You will train the model on our dataset. We need to define the number of epochs, which is the number of times the training algorithm will iterate over the entire dataset.

```
model.fit(square_footage, house_prices, epochs=1000)
```

Evaluating the Model

After training, we can evaluate the model using some test data.

```
test_square_footage = np.array([1200, 1800])
test_house_prices = np.array([120000, 180000])

model.evaluate(test_square_footage, test_house_prices)
```

Making Predictions

We can now use the trained model to predict house prices for any given square footage.

```
new_square_footage = np.array([2200])
predicted_price = model.predict(new_square_footage)
print(f"The predicted price for a {new_square_footage[0]} square foot house is {predicted_price[0][0]}")
```

Visualizing the Results

For linear regression, it is helpful to visualize the relationship. We can plot the original data along with the model's predictions.

```
import matplotlib.pyplot as plt

predicted_prices = model.predict(square_footage)
plt.scatter(square_footage, house_prices, color='blue')
plt.plot(square_footage, predicted_prices, color='red')
plt.xlabel('Square Footage')
plt.ylabel('Price')
plt.show()
```

In the given example, we utilized a neural network to execute straightforward linear regression tasks. While this may appear to be a rudimentary application, it serves as a compelling illustration of the neural network's ability to capture even elementary data relationships. Grasping the mechanics of this example serves as a foundational step for venturing into more intricate models and diverse applications. This above example acts as an initial milestone in harnessing the full potential of neural networks for addressing multifaceted challenges in a variety of fields. By focusing on linear relationships, this example also offers you an insightful perspective into how neural networks can seamlessly integrate with traditional statistical methods, thereby forming a cohesive link between time-honored statistical techniques and cutting-edge deep learning methodologies.

Gradient Descent: A Closer Look

As we delve further into the realm of neural networks, it becomes imperative to focus on Gradient Descent, a key algorithm that orchestrates the training process. Although we've briefly mentioned it before, a more comprehensive examination is essential for grasping how it empowers neural networks to learn effectively from datasets.

What is Gradient Descent?

Gradient Descent serves as an optimization technique whose primary objective is to identify the function's minimum value. Within the framework of neural networks, this function is commonly known as the loss or cost function. This function quantifies the discrepancy between the model's predictions and the actual target values.

How Does Gradient Descent Work?

The core principle behind Gradient Descent is iterative optimization. It aims to move step-by-step in the direction where the function experiences the most significant rate of decrease, which is essentially opposite to the direction of the gradient.

Computing the Gradient

In mathematical terms, the gradient is the vector of partial derivatives of the loss function with respect to each weight and bias within the neural network. This vector points in the direction where the loss function experiences its steepest ascent.

Updating Parameters

The weights and biases in the neural network are adjusted in a direction that is antithetical to the gradient. This adjustment is a function of both the negative gradient and the learning rate, ensuring that the model iteratively moves towards minimizing the loss function.

Learning Rate

The learning rate is a crucial hyperparameter that influences the magnitude of each step taken during the iterative process of Gradient Descent. A learning rate that is too small will result in a sluggish convergence towards the minimum, making the training process inefficient. Conversely, an excessively large learning rate can cause the model to oscillate wildly or even diverge, thereby failing to find the optimal solution.

Understanding the gradient descent's geometric interpretation helps in choosing the right type and tuning the parameters. In sum, Gradient Descent is more than an optimization algorithm; it's the engine that drives the learning process in neural networks. From its basic concepts to advanced variants, understanding Gradient Descent is crucial for anyone working with neural networks or other machine learning models. Its flexible nature allows it to be adapted and fine-tuned to various tasks, reflecting its central role in the evolving field of artificial intelligence.

Computational Graphs

Expanding on our prior section about gradient descent, the concept of Computational Graphs emerges as a crucial element for effective gradient computation and optimization in the realm of deep learning. This concept is integral to both the architecture and functionality of deep learning platforms such as TensorFlow.

What are Computational Graphs?

A computational graph serves as a directed graph in which the nodes symbolize operations or variables, and the edges signify the flow of data between these nodes. Within the context of deep learning, computational graphs act as the structural framework of neural networks, illustrating the flow of data as it traverses through multiple layers and undergoes various transformations.

Components of a Computational Graph

- Nodes: These are the vertices of the graph, each representing a specific mathematical operation, such as addition, multiplication, or activation functions like ReLU and Sigmoid.

- Edges: These are the connecting lines between nodes, representing the tensors that flow from one operation to another.

- Input Nodes: These nodes stand for the initial data or parameters that are fed into the network, such as weights and biases.

- Output Nodes: These nodes denote the final outcome or prediction generated by the neural network.

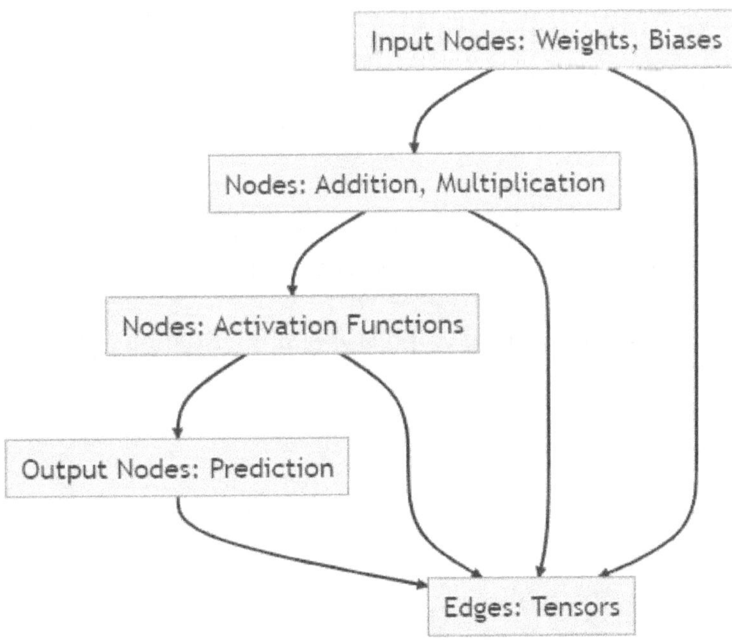

Fig 2.1 Components - Computational Graphs

How Computational Graphs Work?

- Forward Pass: During this phase, data is propagated through the graph, with each node executing its corresponding operation in a sequential manner.

- Backward Pass: In this phase, gradients are calculated using the backpropagation algorithm, essentially traversing the graph in the opposite direction to adjust the weights and biases.

Why use Computational Graphs?

- Modularity: Computational graphs offer the advantage of constructing intricate models by piecing together simpler components. This modular approach makes it more straightforward to design, debug, and update neural network models.

- Efficiency: The structure of computational graphs allows for parallel execution across multiple hardware resources, leading to optimized performance. Additionally, the graph itself can be optimized for more efficient execution.

- Automatic Differentiation: Computational graphs facilitate automatic differentiation via backpropagation, which is essential for gradient-based optimization techniques like gradient descent.

Types of Computational Graphs

- Static Computational Graphs: These graphs are defined once and then executed multiple times. While this approach offers more opportunities for optimization, it comes at the cost of reduced flexibility.

- Dynamic Computational Graphs: In this case, the graph is defined and executed on-the-fly. This offers greater flexibility at the potential expense of efficiency.

In TensorFlow, defining a computational graph is as simple as defining the operations:

```
import tensorflow as tf

# Define operations
a = tf.constant(5)
b = tf.constant(3)
c = tf.add(a, b)
d = tf.multiply(a, b)
```

```
# Execute graph
with tf.Session() as sess:
    print(sess.run([c, d]))
```

Computational graphs have become a foundational concept in deep learning, influencing how models are built, trained, and deployed. By providing a structured, visual representation of mathematical operations, they enable more efficient computation and provide a clear path for the application of optimization algorithms. Whether defining the forward pass of a neural network, calculating gradients during backpropagation, or optimizing for execution across hardware, computational graphs play a central role in modern deep learning. Understanding this concept helps in leveraging the power of modern deep learning frameworks to their fullest, and provides insights into the underlying mechanics that make deep learning both powerful and accessible.

Sample Program: Computational Graphs in TensorFlow

Continuing from our theoretical understanding of computational graphs, let us delve into a practical demonstration of how computational graphs work within TensorFlow.

In TensorFlow, everything is built on the computational graph concept. This graph consists of nodes (operations) and edges (tensors) that outline how computations are executed.

Building a Simple Graph

Let us begin by defining a simple graph that adds two numbers:

```
import tensorflow as tf

# Define two constants
a = tf.constant(5, name="a")
b = tf.constant(3, name="b")

# Define addition operation
addition = tf.add(a, b, name="addition")
```

Here, a and b are nodes representing constants, and addition is a node representing the addition operation. The name argument helps in visualizing the graph later.

Executing the Graph using Session

To execute the graph, you need to create a TensorFlow session:

```
# Create a session
with tf.Session() as sess:
    print(sess.run(addition))  # Output: 8
```

A session is a runtime environment where operations are executed, and tensors are evaluated.

Visualizing the Graph with TensorBoard

TensorFlow provides a utility called TensorBoard for visualizing computational graphs:

```
# Create a summary writer
writer = tf.summary.FileWriter('./logs', tf.get_default_graph())

# Close the writer
writer.close()
```

Running tensorboard --logdir="./logs" in the command line will open TensorBoard, where you can see the graph.

```
# Resetting the graph
tf.reset_default_graph()

# Define placeholder and variable
x = tf.placeholder(tf.float32, name="x")
W = tf.Variable([2.0], dtype=tf.float32, name="W")
b = tf.Variable([-1.0], dtype=tf.float32, name="b")

# Define linear model
linear_model = W * x + b
```

```
# Initialize variables
init = tf.global_variables_initializer()

# Run the graph
with tf.Session() as sess:
    sess.run(init)
    print(sess.run(linear_model, {x: [1, 2, 3, 4]})) # Output: [ 1.  3.  5.  7.]
```

By exploring computational graphs in TensorFlow, from simple mathematical operations to complex neural networks, you get a practical understanding of how this concept powers the entire workflow within the framework. This understanding is foundational in working with TensorFlow, whether you're building a basic linear regression model or a complex deep learning system. From the building and execution of graphs to visualization and advanced functionalities, TensorFlow leverages computational graphs to provide a versatile, powerful platform for all kinds of machine learning and deep learning tasks.

Perform Convolutional Operations

Continuing from our exploration of computational graphs in TensorFlow, let us move into the practical aspects of performing convolutional operations. Convolutional operations are crucial in the processing of image data and form the basis of Convolutional Neural Networks (CNNs).

Convolutional operations apply filters to an input image to detect features like edges, textures, and patterns. These operations play a vital role in image recognition tasks.

In TensorFlow, the tf.nn.conv2d function is used to perform 2D convolutional operations.

Following is a step-by-step walkthrough to practically understanding this concept:

Preparing the Input

First, you need to prepare the input image and filter (kernel). Let us take a simple example with a 5x5 grayscale image and a 3x3 filter:

```
import tensorflow as tf
import numpy as np

# 5x5 image with one channel (grayscale)
```

```
image = np.array([[1, 2, 3, 4, 5],
                  [5, 6, 7, 8, 9],
                  [9, 10, 11, 12, 13],
                  [13, 14, 15, 16, 17],
                  [17, 18, 19, 20, 21]], dtype=np.float32)

# Reshaping image to match TensorFlow's input shape (batch_size, height, width,
channels)
image = image.reshape(1, 5, 5, 1)

# 3x3 filter (kernel)
filter = np.array([[1, 2, 1],
                   [0, 0, 0],
                   [-1, -2, -1]], dtype=np.float32)

# Reshaping filter to match TensorFlow's input shape (height, width, input_channels,
output_channels)
filter = filter.reshape(3, 3, 1, 1)
```

Defining the Convolutional Operation

Now, you will use tf.nn.conv2d to perform the convolution:

```
# Convert image and filter to tensors
input_image = tf.constant(image)
conv_filter = tf.constant(filter)

# Apply convolution
convolution = tf.nn.conv2d(input_image, conv_filter, strides=[1, 1, 1, 1],
padding='VALID')
```

Here, strides determine how the filter moves across the image, and padding controls whether the image boundaries are extended to fit the filter.

Executing the Convolution

Let us execute the operation in a TensorFlow session:

```
with tf.Session() as sess:
    output = sess.run(convolution)
    print(output)
```

Understanding the Output

The output is a 3x3 feature map, showing how the filter responded to different regions of the image. This specific filter detects vertical edges.

Convolutional operations form the core of image processing in deep learning, enabling the network to learn and recognize complex patterns and features within the data. By understanding and practicing these operations in TensorFlow, you get the foundational knowledge necessary to work on intricate image recognition tasks, whether you're building a simple model to recognize shapes or a complex system to detect objects in real-time.

Summary

In this chapter, we delved into the detailed aspects of neural networks, including their components and practical implementations. Starting with an in-depth exploration of neural networks, we understood the architecture comprising input layers, hidden layers, and output layers, along with activation functions. We also learned about various types of neural networks like feedforward, recurrent, and convolutional neural networks.

Following this foundation, we applied neural networks to perform simple linear regression analysis. By demonstrating how to construct and train a network, we showcased how neural networks could replicate traditional statistical methods. We then explored gradient descent, a fundamental optimization algorithm used to minimize the error in neural networks, explaining how it works in detail.

The latter part of the chapter focused on computational graphs and their functionality within deep learning. We explained the benefits of using computational graphs and demonstrated how TensorFlow utilizes them for efficient execution. This section was enriched with practical examples and code snippets. Finally, we explored convolutional operations, diving into their theory and application in TensorFlow, with emphasis on image processing. We covered everything from basic convolutional operations to building a Convolutional Neural Network (CNN), implementing activation functions, and using pre-trained models.

Overall, this chapter provided a comprehensive view of the essential components of neural networks and their practical application using TensorFlow. You would have gained hands-on experience and theoretical insights, empowering them to take on more complex deep learning challenges.

CHAPTER 3: BUILDING BASIC MACHINE LEARNING MODELS

Supervised and Unsupervised Learning

Supervised Learning is characterized by the presence of labeled data. In this approach, the model is trained on a dataset containing input-output pairs, where the output, or label, is known. The model learns to map inputs to the correct outputs by minimizing the error between its predictions and the actual labels. This learning process is supervised, meaning that the model is guided by the correct answers. Common supervised learning algorithms include regression, classification, support vector machines, and neural networks.

Contrastingly, Unsupervised Learning deals with data that has not been labeled. The model is left to find patterns, structures, and relationships within the data on its own without any guidance. Unlike supervised learning, where the model learns to predict specific outputs, unsupervised learning aims to discover hidden structures. Clustering and dimensionality reduction are examples of tasks tackled by unsupervised learning methods, such as k-means clustering or Principal Component Analysis (PCA).

The distinction between supervised and unsupervised learning manifests in various aspects of model construction, training, and application:

- In supervised learning, the objective is to predict specific outputs based on inputs. In unsupervised learning, the goal is to discover underlying structures within the data.

- Supervised learning requires labeled data, where the correct output for each input is known. Unsupervised learning, on the other hand, works with unlabeled data and finds patterns without guidance.

- Supervised learning algorithms often entail a more complex training process, as they need to fine-tune the model parameters to predict the labels accurately. Unsupervised learning algorithms may be simpler since they are not constrained by specific output predictions.

- Evaluating a supervised learning model is generally more straightforward since the correct outputs are known. Metrics like accuracy, precision, and recall can be used. In unsupervised learning, evaluation is more subjective, and domain knowledge may be required to assess the quality of the discovered patterns.

- Supervised learning is employed when there's a specific prediction task, such as spam email detection or house price prediction. Unsupervised learning is used for exploratory analysis, clustering customers, or reducing the dimensions of high-dimensional data.

- Supervised learning models may offer more interpretability since the relationship between inputs and outputs can be examined. Unsupervised learning models might be more challenging to interpret due to the lack of explicit guidance in the learning process.

- Unsupervised learning allows for more creativity and exploration, as the model is not bound by specific output constraints. Supervised learning models are more directed towards achieving specific predictive goals.

The dichotomy between supervised and unsupervised learning lies in the presence or absence of guidance during the learning process, the complexity of the algorithms, the requirements of the data, the goals of the modeling, and the methods used for evaluation. These differences dictate the choice of approach in various real-world applications and research, underlining the importance of understanding both paradigms deeply. Whether predicting future outcomes or discovering unseen patterns, the intricate balance between supervised and unsupervised learning continues to shape the frontier of machine learning and artificial intelligence.

Sample Program: Classification Model

Let us delve into a hands-on illustration of constructing a model for classification tasks. In the realm of supervised learning, classification aims to assign predefined categorical labels to new data points, drawing insights from historical data. This practical example will offer a step-by-step walkthrough on how to build a robust classification model effectively.

For our demonstration, you will use the famous Iris dataset, which is readily available in several libraries like Scikit-Learn. The dataset consists of 150 samples of iris flowers, with four features each: sepal length, sepal width, petal length, and petal width. The task is to classify the iris flowers into one of three species: Setosa, Versicolor, or Virginica.

You can also find the dataset at the following URL:
https://archive.ics.uci.edu/dataset/53/iris

Loading the Data

You will start by loading the Iris dataset. If you're using Python and Scikit-Learn, you can easily load it with the following code:

```
from sklearn.datasets import load_iris
data = load_iris()
X, y = data.data, data.target
```

Exploratory Data Analysis

Understanding your data is crucial. You might want to visualize it using libraries like Matplotlib or Seaborn, or describe it using Pandas to understand the distributions, correlations, and potential preprocessing needs.

```
import pandas as pd
df = pd.DataFrame(data=X, columns=data.feature_names)
df['target'] = y
print(df.head())
```

Splitting the Data

You will split the data into training and testing sets to evaluate the model's performance.

```
from sklearn.model_selection import train_test_split
X_train, X_test, y_train, y_test = train_test_split(X, y, test_size=0.2, random_state=42)
```

Building the Model

You will use a simple logistic regression classifier for this task.

```
from sklearn.linear_model import LogisticRegression
model = LogisticRegression(max_iter=200)
model.fit(X_train, y_train)
```

Evaluating the Model

Once the model is trained, we can evaluate its performance on the test set.

```
from sklearn.metrics import accuracy_score
predictions = model.predict(X_test)
accuracy = accuracy_score(y_test, predictions)
print(f'Accuracy: {accuracy}')
```

Making Predictions

You can now use this trained model to make predictions on new data points.

```
new_data = [[5.1, 3.5, 1.4, 0.2]]
prediction = model.predict(new_data)
print(f'Predicted class: {data.target_names[prediction]}')
```

By adhering to the outlined procedures, you'll construct a straightforward classification model leveraging the Iris dataset. This demonstration walks you through essential steps such as data loading, preliminary exploratory data analysis, partitioning the dataset into training and test subsets, model construction, evaluation, and ultimately, prediction-making. The methodologies and tools showcased in the above sample program serve as the bedrock for a multitude of advanced machine learning endeavors. Therefore, this exercise is invaluable for individuals aiming to gain a more profound understanding of supervised learning and classification techniques.

Model Evaluation and Metrics

Building upon the previous demonstration where we created a classification model, you will now explore model evaluation and various metrics in detail. Evaluating a model's performance is as crucial as building it, as it allows us to understand how well the model is performing and where improvements can be made.

Model Metrics

Accuracy

Accuracy is a straightforward metric that calculates the proportion of correct predictions in relation to the total number of predictions made. While it provides a quick snapshot of the model's performance, it is most effective when used on balanced datasets. In cases where the class distribution is skewed, relying solely on accuracy can be misleading.

Precision

Precision is a metric that focuses on the quality of the positive predictions made by the model. It is calculated by dividing the number of true positive predictions by the sum of true positives and false positives. This metric is particularly useful in scenarios where the cost of false positives is high, such as in medical diagnosis or spam detection.

Recall

Also known as Sensitivity, Recall measures the model's ability to correctly identify all relevant instances. It is calculated by dividing the number of true positives by the sum of true positives and false negatives. This metric is crucial in situations where missing a positive instance has significant consequences, like in fraud detection.

F1-Score

The F1-Score is the harmonic mean of Precision and Recall, aiming to balance the two metrics. It is especially useful when you want a single metric that considers both false positives and false negatives. The F1-Score is often more informative than accuracy, especially for imbalanced datasets.

ROC-AUC

The Receiver Operating Characteristic curve (ROC) is a graphical representation that plots the true positive rate against the false positive rate at various threshold settings. The Area Under the Curve (AUC) condenses the ROC curve into a single scalar value, offering an aggregate measure of the model's ability to distinguish between positive and negative classes across different thresholds.

Confusion Matrix

A confusion matrix is a table that provides a more granular view of the model's performance. It categorizes predictions into four types: true positives, false positives, true negatives, and false negatives. This matrix is invaluable for understanding the type of errors your model is making.

Mean Absolute Error (MAE) and Mean Squared Error (MSE

For tasks that involve regression rather than classification, Mean Absolute Error (MAE) and Mean Squared Error (MSE) are commonly used. MAE measures the average of the absolute differences between predicted and actual values, giving an idea of the magnitude of the errors without considering their direction. On the other hand, MSE squares the errors before averaging them, which penalizes larger errors more severely.

Applying Evaluation Metrics

Let us evaluate our logistic regression model trained on the Iris dataset using some of the above metrics:

```
from sklearn.metrics import accuracy_score, precision_score, recall_score, f1_score,
confusion_matrix, roc_auc_score
from sklearn.preprocessing import label_binarize

# Accuracy
accuracy = accuracy_score(y_test, predictions)
print(f'Accuracy: {accuracy}')

# Precision, Recall, F1-Score
precision = precision_score(y_test, predictions, average='macro')
recall = recall_score(y_test, predictions, average='macro')
f1 = f1_score(y_test, predictions, average='macro')
print(f'Precision: {precision}, Recall: {recall}, F1-Score: {f1}')
```

```
# Confusion Matrix
conf_matrix = confusion_matrix(y_test, predictions)
print(f'Confusion Matrix:\n{conf_matrix}')

# ROC-AUC (Multi-class needs binarization)
y_test_binarized = label_binarize(y_test, classes=[0, 1, 2])
predictions_binarized = label_binarize(predictions, classes=[0, 1, 2])
roc_auc = roc_auc_score(y_test_binarized, predictions_binarized, average='macro')
print(f'ROC-AUC: {roc_auc}')
```

The above code snippet will provide you with an in-depth evaluation of the model using various metrics. Understanding these metrics and applying them appropriately gives you insights into the model's strengths and weaknesses.

Optimization Techniques

Optimization techniques are vital in training deep learning models, as they determine how the model's parameters are updated during training to minimize the loss function. These techniques influence the speed of convergence, the final model quality, and sometimes even the entire training dynamics. Below are some of the common optimization techniques, each with unique characteristics and applications.

Gradient Descent

Gradient Descent serves as the bedrock for a plethora of optimization techniques in machine learning. It aims to minimize the loss function by iteratively adjusting the model's parameters in the direction that reduces the gradient of the loss function. The mathematical representation of the update rule is:

$$\theta=\theta-\eta\nabla J(\theta)$$

Here, θ symbolizes the model's parameters, η denotes the learning rate, and $\nabla J(\theta)$ represents the gradient of the loss function J with respect to θ.

Stochastic Gradient Descent (SGD)

Stochastic Gradient Descent is a variation of the basic Gradient Descent algorithm that updates the model's parameters using just a single data point at each iteration. While this approach can be computationally faster and has the potential to escape local minima, it introduces more noise into the optimization process, making it less stable compared to its batch counterpart.

Mini-Batch Gradient Descent

Mini-Batch Gradient Descent offers a compromise between Batch Gradient Descent and Stochastic Gradient Descent. It updates the model's parameters using a small, randomly-selected subset of the training data. This hybrid approach combines the computational advantages of SGD with the more stable and convergent behavior of Batch Gradient Descent.

Momentum

Momentum enhances the Stochastic Gradient Descent algorithm by adding a component of the previous gradient to the current one. This dampens oscillations and propels the algorithm along relevant directions, thereby potentially accelerating the convergence rate. Mathematically, it introduces a velocity term that accumulates the gradient of the loss function over time.

Nesterov Accelerated Gradient (NAG)

Nesterov Accelerated Gradient is an advanced form of Momentum that calculates the gradient a step ahead in the direction of the accumulated gradient. This lookahead feature often results in more informed updates, thereby improving the optimization process.

Adagrad

Adagrad dynamically adjusts the learning rate during the training process. It scales down the learning rate for features that occur frequently and scales it up for less common features. This adaptive behavior is particularly beneficial in scenarios involving sparse data sets, such as natural language processing tasks.

RMSprop

RMSprop (Root Mean Square Propagation) is an extension of Adagrad that mitigates some of its shortcomings by using a moving average of the squared gradients to normalize the gradient. This results in different learning rates for each parameter and often leads to better performance, especially in non-convex optimization landscapes.

Adam

Adam (Adaptive Moment Estimation) is a sophisticated optimization algorithm that amalgamates the strengths of both Momentum and RMSprop. It maintains an exponentially decaying average of past gradients and past squared gradients. This hybrid approach has proven to be effective across a wide array of machine learning problems, from simple linear regression to complex neural networks.

The choice of the optimizer depends on the specific problem, the data, the model architecture, and even empirical trial and error. Some optimizers might work better for certain types of data or models.

Sample Program: Model Optimization

Referring to our one of the previous sample programs about creating a classification model using the Iris dataset, let us delve into the practical application of the Adam optimization algorithm. Adam, an acronym for Adaptive Moment Estimation, is a highly versatile optimization technique that amalgamates the strengths of two other prominent algorithms: Momentum and RMSprop.

In the context of our Iris dataset classification model, employing Adam can offer several advantages. For instance, Adam's adaptive learning rate adjustment can be particularly useful when dealing with multi-dimensional feature spaces, as is the case with the Iris dataset. Additionally, the momentum component helps the algorithm navigate through the parameter space more efficiently, potentially leading to quicker convergence.

Define the Model

Assuming you have defined a classification model with several layers, let us say a simple feed-forward neural network for binary classification. Following is a reminder of the basic structure:

```
import tensorflow as tf

model = tf.keras.Sequential([
    tf.keras.layers.Dense(128, activation='relu', input_shape=(input_shape,)),
    tf.keras.layers.Dense(64, activation='relu'),
    tf.keras.layers.Dense(1, activation='sigmoid')
])
```

Define the Adam Optimizer

The Adam optimizer is popular because it is robust to the choice of hyperparameters and often works well with default settings. Following is how you can define the Adam optimizer in TensorFlow:

```
adam_optimizer = tf.keras.optimizers.Adam(learning_rate=0.001)
```

The learning rate 0.001 is a common choice, but you can tune this hyperparameter according to your specific problem.

Compile Model with Adam Optimizer

Next, you'll need to compile your model using the defined optimizer, specifying the loss function and metrics to track:

```
model.compile(optimizer=adam_optimizer,
        loss='binary_crossentropy',
        metrics=['accuracy'])
```

Load and Preprocess the Data

Assuming you've already loaded your dataset, make sure it is split into training and validation sets, and preprocessed as needed for your specific problem.

Train the Model

Finally, train the model using the fit method:

```
history = model.fit(X_train, y_train,
           epochs=10,
           batch_size=32,
           validation_data=(X_val, y_val))
```

Here, X_train and y_train are your training features and labels, and X_val and y_val are your validation features and labels.

Evaluate and Analyze

After training, you can evaluate the model on a test set, analyze the training history, visualize loss and accuracy curves, etc. This would provide insights into how the Adam optimizer has performed compared to other optimization techniques. Its adaptive learning rate capabilities make it suitable for a wide range of problems. By incorporating Adam into your training, you can potentially achieve faster convergence and better model performance.

This above practical example illustrates how easy it is to apply the Adam optimizer using TensorFlow, and the same approach can be used to explore other optimizers and compare their performances on your specific problem.

Save and Load Models

Saving and loading models is an essential part of the machine learning workflow, especially in deep learning where training can take a considerable amount of time. In the context of the previous example using TensorFlow, let us explore the process of saving and loading models.

Saving a Trained Model

After you've trained your model using the Adam optimizer as demonstrated earlier, you may want to save it to disk so that you can reload it later, without having to retrain it. Below is how to do that in TensorFlow.

Saving the Entire Model

You can save the entire model, including the optimizer, architecture, weights, and even the training configuration. Here's how:

```
# Save the entire model as a SavedModel.
model.save('path/to/location')
```

Saving Only the Weights

If you want to save only the weights of the model:

```
# Save the weights
model.save_weights('path/to/location/weights')
```

Saving the Architecture

To save only the architecture of the model:

```
# Save the architecture
json_config = model.to_json()
with open('path/to/location/architecture.json', 'w') as json_file:
    json_file.write(json_config)
```

Loading a Saved Model

Now that you've saved your model, you can load it back at any time. Below is how to do that:

Loading the Entire Model

If you saved the entire model, you can load it back including its architecture, weights, and even the optimizer state:

```
# Load the entire model
loaded_model = tf.keras.models.load_model('path/to/location')
```

Loading Only the Weights

If you saved only the weights, you'll need to define the model architecture again before loading the weights:

```
# Define the model architecture (as before)
model = create_model() # Assuming create_model returns the previously defined model

# Load the weights
model.load_weights('path/to/location/weights')
```

Loading the Architecture

If you saved the architecture separately, you can load it as follows:

```
# Load the architecture
with open('path/to/location/architecture.json', 'r') as json_file:
    json_config = json_file.read()

# Reinitialize the model
loaded_model = tf.keras.models.model_from_json(json_config)

# Optionally, load the weights if they were saved separately
loaded_model.load_weights('path/to/location/weights')
```

Saving and loading models is an essential aspect of the deep learning workflow, and TensorFlow provides multiple ways to achieve this. You can save the entire model, including its architecture, weights, and training configuration, or you can save only the parts you need. It's important to remember that when you're loading a saved model back into your environment, consistency is crucial. The loading process needs to align with how the model was initially saved. For instance, if you saved the entire model, you'll need to load it in the same manner to ensure that all components, including architecture, weights, and training configurations, are accurately restored.

Summary

In this chapter, the exploration began with a brief overview of supervised and unsupervised learning, emphasizing their differences and the distinct model structures for each. The intricacies of classification models were discussed, followed by a step-by-step demonstration of building a simple classification model. A vital part of the machine learning process, model evaluation, and metrics, was thoroughly explained, providing insights into assessing model performance.

Following the model development and evaluation, optimization techniques became a focal point. The Adam optimization technique was particularly highlighted, with an example demonstrating its application to the previous classification model. Its merits over other optimization techniques were also discussed, revealing its wide adoption in the field of deep learning.

The chapter then transitioned into practical TensorFlow components, delving into computational graphs and their benefits in deep learning. A hands-on example showed how to construct and execute computational graphs using TensorFlow. Continuing on the practical path, convolutional operations were explored in depth, imparting the ability to understand and perform these essential tasks within deep learning.

Finally, the vital practice of saving and loading models was elucidated, providing step-by-step instructions for various scenarios. Whether saving the entire model, only the weights, or the architecture, the techniques and considerations were detailed, ensuring a robust understanding of this critical aspect of deep learning. These methods allow for better workflow management, time savings, and collaboration, fortifying the comprehensive grasp of TensorFlow and deep learning provided in this chapter.

Chapter 4: Image Recognition with Convolutional Neural Networks (CNN)

Building CNNs from Scratch

Creating a Convolutional Neural Network (CNN) from the ground up is an essential competency for anyone aspiring to excel in the field of deep learning, particularly for tasks related to image processing. CNNs have become the go-to architecture for a multitude of applications, ranging from image recognition and object detection to medical image analysis and autonomous vehicle systems. Understanding the intricacies of CNNs provides a strong foundation for tackling complex image-based problems.

CNNs have gained immense popularity due to their unparalleled performance in handling image data. Unlike traditional machine learning algorithms, CNNs are adept at automatically and adaptively learning spatial hierarchies of features, making them highly efficient for image classification, object detection, image segmentation, and even video analysis. Their ability to learn from the texture, shape, and arrangement of visual elements in an image makes them incredibly versatile and effective.

For the purpose of this practice, you will be utilizing the Fashion MNIST dataset, an open-source collection that includes grayscale images of various clothing items such as shirts, trousers, and dresses.

Import Libraries and Load Dataset

The Fashion MNIST dataset is readily available in TensorFlow's keras module. First, you will import the necessary libraries and load the dataset.

```
import tensorflow as tf
from tensorflow.keras.datasets import fashion_mnist

# Load Fashion MNIST dataset
(train_images, train_labels), (test_images, test_labels) = fashion_mnist.load_data()
```

You can find more details about the dataset in the following URL: https://github.com/zalandoresearch/fashion-mnist

Preprocess the Data

The images in the Fashion MNIST dataset are grayscale, with pixel values ranging from 0 to 255. We need to normalize these values to the range [0,1].

```
train_images, test_images = train_images / 255.0, test_images / 255.0
```

Build the CNN Architecture

A typical CNN architecture consists of Convolutional layers, followed by Pooling layers, and then fully connected Dense layers.

```
model = tf.keras.Sequential([
    tf.keras.layers.Reshape((28, 28, 1), input_shape=(28, 28)),
    tf.keras.layers.Conv2D(32, (3,3), activation='relu'),
    tf.keras.layers.MaxPooling2D((2, 2)),
    tf.keras.layers.Conv2D(64, (3,3), activation='relu'),
    tf.keras.layers.MaxPooling2D((2, 2)),
    tf.keras.layers.Conv2D(64, (3,3), activation='relu'),
    tf.keras.layers.Flatten(),
    tf.keras.layers.Dense(64, activation='relu'),
    tf.keras.layers.Dense(10, activation='softmax')
])
```

Compile the Model

Before training, we need to compile the model, specifying the optimizer, loss function, and metrics to monitor.

```
model.compile(optimizer='adam',
              loss='sparse_categorical_crossentropy',
              metrics=['accuracy'])
```

Train the Model

You will now train the model using the training images and labels.

```
model.fit(train_images, train_labels, epochs=10)
```

Evaluate the Model

Finally, you will evaluate the model's performance using the test images and labels.

```
test_loss, test_acc = model.evaluate(test_images, test_labels)
```

```
print('Test accuracy:', test_acc)
```

This detailed walkthrough serves as an instructive handbook for constructing a Convolutional Neural Network (CNN) using TensorFlow, specifically by leveraging the widely-used Fashion MNIST dataset. As you journey through each carefully outlined step, you'll gain an in-depth understanding of the foundational elements that constitute a CNN. This includes every stage of the model's life cycle, starting with the initial phase of data preprocessing, moving on to the architectural design of the neural network, and concluding with the assessment and evaluation of the model's performance.

Pre-processing of Images

Image preprocessing stands as an indispensable phase in the construction of a Convolutional Neural Network (CNN), often serving as the linchpin for enhancing the overall performance of the model. This crucial step aims to refine the quality and interpretability of the input images, thereby enabling the neural network to more efficiently and accurately learn the essential features embedded within the visual data. The primary goal of image preprocessing is to transform the raw image data into a format that is more amenable to analysis by the subsequent layers of the CNN. By doing so, the model is better equipped to focus on the salient features of the image, such as edges, textures, and color distributions, while minimizing the impact of noise and other irrelevant variations. This, in turn, often leads to a more robust and accurate model that can generalize well to new, unseen data.

The importance of image preprocessing cannot be overstated. In many real-world applications, the raw image data is often plagued by various issues such as inconsistent lighting, varying scales, and orientations, or even occlusions. Preprocessing techniques like normalization, resizing, and data augmentation can mitigate these issues, thereby providing the CNN with a cleaner, more standardized dataset to learn from. When executed effectively, image preprocessing can have a cascading positive impact on the entire machine learning pipeline. Not only does it improve the training efficiency by reducing the computational burden, but it also often results in models that require fewer layers or nodes to achieve similar or better performance metrics, thereby making the network more computationally efficient during both training and inference stages.

Following is an in-depth look at various preprocessing techniques commonly used for CNNs.

Scaling: Standardizing Image Dimensions

In Convolutional Neural Networks, it's crucial to have input images of consistent dimensions. Scaling or resizing images to a common size can be accomplished using various interpolation techniques such as bilinear, bicubic, and nearest-neighbor methods.

```
from skimage.transform import resize
image_resized = resize(image, (256, 256))
```

Normalization: Stabilizing Pixel Intensity

Normalization is another fundamental preprocessing step that involves converting pixel values to a specific range, usually [0,1]. This not only speeds up the convergence of the model but also contributes to the stability of the training process.

```
image_normalized = image.astype('float32') / 255.0
```

Data Augmentation: Enhancing Dataset Diversity

Data augmentation is a technique used to artificially expand the training dataset, thereby making the model more robust and capable of generalizing better. Common data augmentation methods include:

Rotation

Rotating the image by a specific angle to introduce variability.

```
from scipy.ndimage import rotate
image_rotated = rotate(image, angle=45)
```

Flipping

Flipping the image either horizontally or vertically to create mirror images.

```
image_flipped = np.fliplr(image)
```

Zooming

Zooming in or out on specific regions of the image to focus on details.

```
from keras.preprocessing.image import ImageDataGenerator
datagen = ImageDataGenerator(zoom_range=0.5)
```

Brightness Adjustment

Modifying the brightness levels to simulate different lighting conditions.

```
from skimage.exposure import adjust_gamma
image_brightened = adjust_gamma(image, gamma=0.5)
```

Exploring Different Color Spaces

Different color spaces like grayscale, HSV, or RGB can capture different types of features. Converting images into these color spaces can provide valuable insights and improve model performance.

```
from skimage.color import rgb2gray, rgb2hsv
image_gray = rgb2gray(image)
image_hsv = rgb2hsv(image)
```

Noise Reduction

Noise reduction techniques like denoising can help the model concentrate on the essential features by eliminating random variations in pixel values.

```
from skimage.restoration import denoise_tv_chambolle
image_denoised = denoise_tv_chambolle(image, weight=0.1)
```

Histogram Equalization

Histogram equalization techniques can improve the contrast of an image, making it easier for the model to identify key features.

```
from skimage.exposure import equalize_hist
image_equalized = equalize_hist(image)
```

Edge Detection

Edge detection techniques like the Sobel filter can be valuable in recognizing the shapes and boundaries of objects within images.

```
from skimage.filters import sobel
image_edges = sobel(image)
```

Batch Processing

Batch processing is essential when dealing with large datasets. It allows for the efficient handling and processing of data chunks, thereby optimizing computational resources.

```
from keras.preprocessing.image import ImageDataGenerator
datagen = ImageDataGenerator()
datagen.fit(images)
```

Geometric Transformations

Geometric transformations like translation, rotation, and shearing can add more variability to the dataset, making the model more robust.

```
from keras.preprocessing.image import ImageDataGenerator
datagen = ImageDataGenerator(shear_range=0.2)
```

By employing these preprocessing techniques, we can make CNNs more versatile and adaptive to various kinds of image data. This thorough insight into image preprocessing equips one with the tools to tune and enhance the performance of CNN models systematically.

Sample Program: MNIST Digit Recognition

The task of recognizing handwritten digits is one of the classic problems in the world of deep learning. It's often used as an entry-point to Convolutional Neural Networks (CNNs). In the below sample program, you will walk through creating a CNN to recognize handwritten digits using the famous MNIST dataset.

Dataset

The MNIST dataset is widely used and contains 60,000 training images and 10,000 testing images of handwritten digits from 0 to 9. The images are 28x28 pixels in size.

You can find the MNIST dataset in the following URL:
https://s3.amazonaws.com/img-datasets/mnist.npz

Alternatively, you can access the MNIST dataset directly through TensorFlow:

```
from tensorflow.keras.datasets import mnist
(train_images, train_labels), (test_images, test_labels) = mnist.load_data()
```

Preprocessing

Before building the model, preprocessing is required. Below is what you'll typically do:

Reshape the Images

Since we're going to use a CNN, the images need to be reshaped to (28, 28, 1).

```
train_images = train_images.reshape((60000, 28, 28, 1))
test_images = test_images.reshape((10000, 28, 28, 1))
```

Normalize the Images

Scale the pixel values down to a range of [0,1].

```
train_images = train_images.astype('float32') / 255
test_images = test_images.astype('float32') / 255
```

Encode the Labels

The labels need to be one-hot encoded.

```
from tensorflow.keras.utils import to_categorical
train_labels = to_categorical(train_labels, 10)
test_labels = to_categorical(test_labels, 10)
```

Model Architecture

Next, you will define the architecture of our CNN:

```
from tensorflow.keras import layers, models

model = models.Sequential()
model.add(layers.Conv2D(32, (3, 3), activation='relu', input_shape=(28, 28, 1)))
model.add(layers.MaxPooling2D((2, 2)))
model.add(layers.Conv2D(64, (3, 3), activation='relu'))
model.add(layers.MaxPooling2D((2, 2)))
model.add(layers.Conv2D(64, (3, 3), activation='relu'))
model.add(layers.Flatten())
```

```
model.add(layers.Dense(64, activation='relu'))
model.add(layers.Dense(10, activation='softmax'))
```

This architecture consists of three convolutional layers followed by max-pooling layers. After flattening, it includes two dense layers with a softmax activation in the last layer.

Compile the Model

After defining the architecture, you need to compile the model:

```
model.compile(optimizer='adam',
        loss='categorical_crossentropy',
        metrics=['accuracy'])
```

Training the Model

Train the model using the training images and labels:

```
model.fit(train_images, train_labels, epochs=5, batch_size=64)
```

Evaluating the Model

Finally, evaluate the model on the test set to see how well it performs:

```
test_loss, test_acc = model.predict(test_images, test_labels)
print('Test Accuracy:', test_acc)
```

This above example provides a comprehensive learning practice to building a CNN for digit recognition using TensorFlow and the MNIST dataset. By following these steps, you can create a robust model capable of recognizing handwritten digits with high accuracy.

LeNet Architecture

Oveview

The LeNet architecture is a pioneering neural network architecture for handwritten and machine-printed character recognition. Proposed by Yann LeCun, Léon Bottou, Yoshua Bengio, and others in 1998, LeNet is one of the earliest convolutional neural networks (CNNs) and has laid down the foundation for deep learning in computer vision.

Input Layer

The LeNet architecture begins with an input layer designed to accept grayscale images. These images are usually resized to a standard dimension of 32x32 pixels, serving as the initial input for the subsequent layers. This uniformity in input size is crucial for maintaining consistency throughout the network.

First Convolutional Layer (C1)

The first convolutional layer, commonly referred to as C1, comprises six convolutional filters or kernels, each with dimensions of 5x5. These filters are convolved with the input image to generate six distinct feature maps, each of size 28x28. The purpose of this layer is to identify basic features in the image like edges and corners.

First Subsampling (Pooling) Layer (S2)

Following the first convolutional layer is the first subsampling or pooling layer, known as S2. This layer employs 2x2 average pooling with a stride of 2 to downsample each of the six 28x28 feature maps generated by C1. The output is six reduced feature maps, each of size 14x14. This layer aids in making the network more computationally efficient and less sensitive to variations in the input.

Second Convolutional Layer (C3)

The second convolutional layer, denoted as C3, takes the six 14x14 feature maps from S2 as its input. It applies 16 convolutional filters, each of size 5x5, to these maps, resulting in 16 new feature maps, each of size 10x10. This layer is responsible for capturing more complex features than the first convolutional layer.

Second Subsampling (Pooling) Layer (S4)

The second subsampling layer, S4, functions similarly to the first subsampling layer, S2. It further reduces the dimensions of the 16 feature maps from C3 to 5x5 each, using 2x2 average pooling with a stride of 2. This layer contributes to the model's ability to generalize well by reducing the computational complexity and the risk of overfitting.

Fully Connected Convolutional Layer (C5)

The sixth layer in the LeNet architecture is a fully connected convolutional layer, labeled as C5. It consists of 120 filters, each of size 5x5. Given that the input feature maps from S4 are also 5x5, this layer produces 120 feature maps of size 1x1. This effectively transforms it into a fully connected layer, serving as a bridge to the subsequent dense layers.

Fully Connected Layer (F6)

The seventh layer, known as F6, is a fully connected or dense layer consisting of 84 units. This layer is fully connected to the preceding C5 layer and serves to integrate the high-level features extracted by the previous layers. It plays a crucial role in the final stages of feature learning within the network.

Output Layer

The architecture concludes with an output layer that is fully connected to the F6 layer. This layer contains as many units as there are classes in the classification problem at hand (for example, 10 units for digit recognition tasks). It usually employs a softmax activation function to produce probability distributions over the classes.

LeNet Implementation in TensorFlow

Following is how you might implement the LeNet architecture using TensorFlow:

```
from tensorflow.keras import layers, models

model = models.Sequential()
model.add(layers.Conv2D(6, (5, 5), activation='tanh', input_shape=(32, 32, 1)))
model.add(layers.AveragePooling2D())
model.add(layers.Conv2D(16, (5, 5), activation='tanh'))
model.add(layers.AveragePooling2D())
model.add(layers.Conv2D(120, (5, 5), activation='tanh'))
model.add(layers.Flatten())
model.add(layers.Dense(84, activation='tanh'))
model.add(layers.Dense(10, activation='softmax'))
```

LeNet was groundbreaking for its time and marked a shift towards using gradient-based learning techniques applied to large neural networks. It was successfully applied to digit recognition tasks, such as reading ZIP codes, digits, etc.

LeNet's design laid the groundwork for many of the concepts that are standard in modern CNNs. Its ideas on hierarchical feature learning, where low-level features like edges and corners are learned in the earlier layers, and high-level features like shapes and patterns are learned in the deeper layers, have become central to CNN design.

Though the architecture seems relatively simple by today's standards, LeNet's principles have guided the design of more complex networks. It remains a valuable educational tool and a starting point for understanding how CNNs work. Though modern architectures have surpassed LeNet in complexity and performance, its underlying concepts continue to influence contemporary deep learning research and applications.

AlexNet Architecture

Overview

AlexNet is another milestone in the history of deep learning and convolutional neural networks. Developed by Alex Krizhevsky, Ilya Sutskever, and Geoffrey Hinton, it won the ImageNet Large Scale Visual Recognition Challenge (ILSVRC) in 2012. AlexNet's revolutionary design and remarkable success played a significant role in bringing deep learning to the forefront of artificial intelligence.

Input Layer

The architecture starts with an input layer designed to receive images of dimensions 224x224 pixels, along with three color channels (Red, Green, and Blue or RGB). This ensures that the network can process high-resolution, color images, making it suitable for a wide range of visual recognition tasks.

First Convolutional Layer (C1)

The first convolutional layer, denoted as C1, is equipped with 96 kernels or filters, each having dimensions of 11x11. These kernels are applied to the input image with a stride of 4, resulting in 96 distinct feature maps. This layer serves as the initial stage for feature extraction, capturing basic elements like edges and textures in the image.

Max Pooling Layer (S1)

Following C1 is the first max pooling layer, labeled as S1. This layer employs a 3x3 window and operates with a stride of 2. The primary function of this layer is to reduce the dimensions of each of the 96 feature maps, making the network more computationally efficient and robust to variations in the input.

Second Convolutional Layer (C2)

The second convolutional layer, known as C2, takes the output from S1 and applies 256 kernels, each of size 5x5. After the convolution operation, a Rectified Linear Unit (ReLU) activation function is applied. This layer is responsible for capturing more complex features compared to C1 and adds non-linearity to the network.

Max Pooling Layer (S2)

Similar to the first max pooling layer, S2 also aims to reduce the dimensions of the feature maps. It operates in a manner akin to S1, further compacting the feature representations and making the network more efficient.

Third to Fifth Convolutional Layers (C3-C5)

These layers, labeled as C3, C4, and C5, contain 384, 384, and 256 filters, respectively. Each filter is of size 3x3. These layers are followed by ReLU activation functions. They are designed to capture highly complex and abstract features, making the network capable of understanding intricate patterns in the input images.

Max Pooling Layer (S3)

The third max pooling layer, S3, serves to further downsample the feature maps generated by the preceding convolutional layers. This contributes to the network's ability to generalize well by reducing the risk of overfitting and computational complexity.

Fully Connected Layers (F6-F8)

The architecture culminates with three fully connected layers, denoted as F6, F7, and F8. These layers contain 4096, 4096, and 1000 neurons, respectively. The final layer, F8, typically employs a softmax activation function to classify the input into one of the 1000 ImageNet classes. These layers serve to integrate the high-level features extracted by the convolutional layers and make the final classification decision.

Normalization and Dropout

To improve the network's performance and robustness, Local Response Normalization (LRN) is applied after the first and second convolutional layers. Additionally, dropout techniques are employed on the fully connected layers to prevent overfitting. This ensures that the network generalizes well to new, unseen data.

AlexNet Implementation in TensorFlow

Below is an example of how AlexNet might be implemented using TensorFlow:

```
from tensorflow.keras import Sequential
from tensorflow.keras.layers import Conv2D, MaxPooling2D, Flatten, Dense, Dropout

model = Sequential([
    Conv2D(96, 11, strides=4, activation='relu', input_shape=(224, 224, 3)),
    MaxPooling2D(3, strides=2),
    Conv2D(256, 5, padding='same', activation='relu'),
    MaxPooling2D(3, strides=2),
    Conv2D(384, 3, padding='same', activation='relu'),
    Conv2D(384, 3, padding='same', activation='relu'),
    Conv2D(256, 3, padding='same', activation='relu'),
    MaxPooling2D(3, strides=2),
```

```
    Flatten(),
    Dense(4096, activation='relu'),
    Dropout(0.5),
    Dense(4096, activation='relu'),
    Dropout(0.5),
    Dense(1000, activation='softmax')
])
```

The primary significance of AlexNet was its capacity to handle a substantial increase in complexity compared to previous models like LeNet. Utilizing ReLU as the activation function and techniques like dropout to minimize overfitting, AlexNet managed to outperform the second-place contestant by more than 10% in the ImageNet challenge. AlexNet spurred a new era of research and investment in deep learning. Many concepts introduced by AlexNet became standards in later architectures.

VGG Architecture

Overview

The VGG (Visual Geometry Group) network is another prominent architecture in the development of Convolutional Neural Networks (CNNs). It was introduced by the Visual Geometry Group at the University of Oxford in 2014 and became known for its simplicity and effectiveness in handling various image recognition tasks.

The VGG architecture comes in different versions, mainly VGG-16 and VGG-19, differing in the number of weight layers they contain (16 and 19, respectively). Following is an overview of the VGG-16 architecture:

Input Layer

The VGG architecture commences its operations by taking an input image of dimensions 224x224 pixels. This image is not grayscale but rather a full-color image, incorporating three color channels: Red, Green, and Blue (RGB). The choice of a 224x224 pixel image with RGB channels allows the network to capture a wide range of features, from basic to complex, across different color spectrums.

Convolutional Layers

One of the most striking features of the VGG architecture is its use of 3x3 convolutional filters with a stride of 1 across all its convolutional layers. This uniformity in filter size contributes to the architecture's elegance and effectiveness in feature extraction.

1. Conv1 Block: This block comprises two layers, each with 64 filters. The use of 64 filters helps in capturing basic features like edges and textures.

2. Conv2 Block: This block also consists of two layers but employs 128 filters to capture more complex features compared to Conv1.

3. Conv3 Block: This block contains three layers, each with 256 filters. The increase in the number of filters allows the network to identify even more intricate patterns.

4. Conv4 Block: Similar to Conv3, this block has three layers but utilizes 512 filters to capture highly complex features and patterns.

5. Conv5 Block: This block mirrors Conv4 in structure, containing three layers with 512 filters each. It serves to further refine the features extracted by the previous layers.

Between each of these convolutional blocks, max pooling is performed using 2x2 windows and a stride of 2. This step reduces the dimensions of the feature maps, making the network more computationally efficient.

Fully Connected Layers

Following the convolutional layers are three fully connected layers that serve as the decision-making components of the architecture.

1. FC1 & FC2: Both of these layers contain a whopping 4096 units each. These layers are responsible for integrating the features extracted by the convolutional layers and preparing them for final classification.

2. FC3: This layer contains 1000 units, corresponding to the number of classes in the ImageNet dataset. It employs a softmax activation function to convert the network's output into probability distributions across the various classes.

ReLU Activation Function

The Rectified Linear Unit (ReLU) activation function is applied immediately after each convolutional and fully connected layer. This introduces non-linearity into the system, allowing the network to learn from the error and make adjustments during backpropagation.

Dropout

To mitigate the risk of overfitting, especially given the network's complexity and depth, dropout is employed after the first two fully connected layers. This involves randomly setting a fraction of input units to zero at each update during training time, which helps to prevent overfitting.

VGG-16 Implementation in TensorFlow

Below is a simplified code snippet demonstrating how VGG-16 can be implemented using TensorFlow:

```
from tensorflow.keras import Sequential
from tensorflow.keras.layers import Conv2D, MaxPooling2D, Flatten, Dense, Dropout

model = Sequential([
    # Block 1
    Conv2D(64, 3, padding='same', activation='relu', input_shape=(224, 224, 3)),
    Conv2D(64, 3, padding='same', activation='relu'),
    MaxPooling2D(2, 2),
    # Block 2
    Conv2D(128, 3, padding='same', activation='relu'),
    Conv2D(128, 3, padding='same', activation='relu'),
    MaxPooling2D(2, 2),
    # Further blocks continue...
    # Fully Connected Layers
    Flatten(),
    Dense(4096, activation='relu'),
    Dropout(0.5),
    Dense(4096, activation='relu'),
    Dropout(0.5),
    Dense(1000, activation='softmax')
])
```

The VGG architecture, particularly VGG-16, became widely recognized for its simplicity, uniformity, and performance. Its structure provided a blueprint for building deep networks, leading to more complex and refined architectures. Though computationally more expensive and demanding more parameters, the VGG architecture demonstrated that depth in a network could translate to higher performance.

Despite newer models overtaking VGG in terms of efficiency and accuracy, VGG's layout and principles continue to influence contemporary deep learning research. It's often used as a base model in various tasks beyond classification, such as object detection and image segmentation. The pre-trained VGG models are widely available and used for transfer learning, a method where a pre-trained model is adapted for a new, different task.

Image Augmentation Techniques

Image augmentation is an essential technique in deep learning, especially in tasks like image recognition and object detection. It refers to the process of creating variations of existing images by applying transformations such as rotation, flipping, scaling, and cropping. The augmented images expand the dataset and introduce diversity, helping the model generalize better and reduce overfitting.

Following is a detailed exploration of image augmentation techniques along with TensorFlow scripts for implementation.

Basic Augmentation Techniques

Flipping: Mirroring the Image

One of the simplest yet effective techniques is flipping the image either horizontally or vertically. This is particularly useful for increasing the diversity of the training set.

```
import tensorflow as tf

def flip_image(image):
    image = tf.image.flip_left_right(image)
    return image
```

Rotation: Changing the Orientation

Rotation involves turning the image by a certain angle. This is useful for making the model invariant to the orientation of the object.

```
def rotate_image(image, angle):
    image = tf.image.rot90(image, k=angle // 90)
    return image
```

Cropping: Extracting Subsections

Cropping is the technique of cutting out a portion of the image. This can be useful for focusing on specific features or objects within the image.

```
def crop_image(image, crop_size):
    image = tf.image.random_crop(image, size=crop_size)
    return image
```

Scaling: Altering Image Dimensions

Scaling involves resizing the image, either making it larger or smaller. This is essential for standardizing the input size for the neural network.

```
def scale_image(image, scale_factor):
    image = tf.image.resize(image, scale_factor)
    return image
```

Advanced Augmentation for Enhanced Performance

Brightness and Contrast Adjustment

Adjusting the brightness and contrast can make the model more robust to varying lighting conditions in the images.

```
def adjust_brightness_contrast(image, brightness_delta, contrast_factor):
    image = tf.image.random_brightness(image, max_delta=brightness_delta)
    image = tf.image.random_contrast(image, lower=1-contrast_factor,
upper=1+contrast_factor)
    return image
```

Saturation and Hue Adjustment: Color Manipulation

Changing the saturation and hue can be beneficial for tasks that are sensitive to color information.

```
def adjust_saturation_hue(image, saturation_factor, hue_delta):
    image = tf.image.random_saturation(image, lower=1-saturation_factor,
upper=1+saturation_factor)
    image = tf.image.random_hue(image, max_delta=hue_delta)
    return image
```

Image Translation: Shifting the Image

Translation involves moving the image along the x or y axis. This can help the model learn to recognize objects that are not perfectly centered.

```
def translate_image(image, translation):
    image = tf.keras.preprocessing.image.apply_affine_transform(image, tx=translation[0],
ty=translation[1])
    return image
```

Integration with TensorFlow Data Pipeline

You can seamlessly integrate these functions into a TensorFlow data pipeline. Below is a code snippet demonstrating how you might combine these augmentations for any given dataset.

```
def image_augmentation(image, label):
    image = flip_image(image)
    image = rotate_image(image, angle=90)
    image = crop_image(image, crop_size=[128, 128, 3])
    image = scale_image(image, scale_factor=[128, 128])
    image = adjust_brightness_contrast(image, brightness_delta=0.1,
contrast_factor=0.2)
    return image, label

train_dataset = train_dataset.map(image_augmentation)
```

These techniques are invaluable for enhancing the performance and robustness of image-based machine learning models. By incorporating these methods into your data preprocessing pipeline, you can significantly improve the model's ability to generalize across diverse and challenging conditions.

Sample Program: Face Recognition

Face recognition is a powerful application of convolutional neural networks (CNNs) that has a variety of uses in security, authentication, and other fields. In this sample program, you will walk through a use case of face recognition using TensorFlow and demonstrate how to incorporate image augmentation techniques learned previously.

Dataset

For practice, the "Labeled Faces in the Wild" (LFW) dataset is widely used for face recognition tasks. It consists of more than 13,000 labeled images of faces collected from the internet.

The dataset can be found in the following URL:
https://vis-www.cs.umass.edu/lfw/

Preprocessing

Before building the model, preprocessing the images is necessary. We need to normalize the pixel values, resize images, and split the data into training and validation sets.

```
from sklearn.model_selection import train_test_split

def preprocess_images(images):
    images = images.astype('float32')
    images /= 255.0
    return images

# Splitting the data
X_train, X_test, y_train, y_test = train_test_split(images, labels, test_size=0.2)

# Preprocessing the images
X_train = preprocess_images(X_train)
X_test = preprocess_images(X_test)
```

Image Augmentation

We can utilize the TensorFlow image augmentation techniques covered previously. Let us use flipping, rotation, and brightness adjustment.

```
def augment_image(image):
    image = flip_image(image)
    image = rotate_image(image, angle=30)
    image = adjust_brightness_contrast(image, brightness_delta=0.1,
contrast_factor=0.2)
    return image

# Apply augmentation to the training data
```

```
X_train = np.array([augment_image(img) for img in X_train])
```

Building the Face Recognition Model

Let us build a convolutional neural network for face recognition. The architecture can be designed with multiple convolutional layers, followed by fully connected layers.

```
from tensorflow.keras.models import Sequential
from tensorflow.keras.layers import Conv2D, MaxPooling2D, Flatten, Dense

model = Sequential([
    Conv2D(32, (3,3), activation='relu', input_shape=(128, 128, 3)),
    MaxPooling2D((2, 2)),
    Conv2D(64, (3,3), activation='relu'),
    MaxPooling2D((2, 2)),
    Conv2D(128, (3,3), activation='relu'),
    MaxPooling2D((2, 2)),
    Flatten(),
    Dense(128, activation='relu'),
    Dense(len(np.unique(labels)), activation='softmax')
])

model.compile(optimizer='adam', loss='sparse_categorical_crossentropy',
metrics=['accuracy'])
```

Training the Model

With the architecture defined, we can train the model using the training data.

```
history = model.fit(X_train, y_train, epochs=10, validation_data=(X_test, y_test))
```

Evaluating the Model

After training, we can evaluate the model's performance on the validation data.

```
loss, accuracy = model.evaluate(X_test, y_test)
```

```
print(f'Validation Accuracy: {accuracy * 100:.2f}%')
```

The above practical steps to face recognition demonstrates how to integrate image preprocessing, augmentation, and CNNs to build a robust face recognition system. Using the LFW dataset, you can explore various architectures and augmentation techniques to further enhance the model.

Summary

In this chapter, the journey began with a detailed exploration of building a convolutional neural network (CNN) from scratch. By examining various pre-processing techniques for images, the groundwork was laid for understanding how to manipulate and prepare data for training neural networks.

Moving forward, the chapter provided practical demonstrations on digit recognition using TensorFlow, diving into renowned architectures like LeNet, AlexNet, and VGG. Each of these architectural explorations presented a more intricate understanding of how layers, activation functions, and other parameters are employed in real-world models. You were guided through understanding the logic behind each design and how these models have shaped modern CNN applications.

The chapter then took a deep dive into image augmentation techniques, an essential part of training robust models. By understanding and implementing these techniques, you learn how to artificially expand the dataset, making models more resilient to overfitting and capable of generalizing better to unseen data. The utilization of TensorFlow scripts for implementing these methods allowed you to grasp their application in a real-world context.

Finally, an extensive demonstration of a face recognition system was presented. Integrating all the previously learned concepts, from data preprocessing to image augmentation and architectural design, this example illustrated the power of CNNs in a practical, relevant application. The systematic, step-by-step walkthrough facilitated a comprehensive understanding of how various parts of deep learning with TensorFlow come together to build a fully functional face recognition system. The provision of code snippets and references to datasets ensures that you have all the necessary tools to experiment and further develop their skills in this fascinating area of deep learning.

CHAPTER 5: OBJECT DETECTION ALGORITHMS

Object Detection: Overview

Object detection is a computer vision task that involves identifying and locating objects within an image or a sequence of images. It's a critical component in various real-world applications, offering both practical and innovative solutions. The following sections provide an in-depth overview of object detection and its wide-ranging applications in production environments.

Basics

Object detection is more than just classifying an object within an image; it also determines the location of the object. This involves identifying the object's bounding box, which delineates the spatial extent of the object. Several object detection algorithms, such as Faster R-CNN, YOLO (You Only Look Once), and SSD (Single Shot MultiBox Detector), have been developed to achieve this task.

Applications

In the healthcare industry, object detection is employed for medical image analysis. Algorithms can identify and locate tumors, fractures, and other abnormalities within medical scans. This automates diagnosis to some extent and assists medical professionals in making more accurate assessments.

Object detection plays a vital role in autonomous vehicles. It helps in identifying and locating other vehicles, pedestrians, signs, and obstacles, enabling the vehicle to navigate safely. It also has applications in traffic monitoring and management by detecting and analyzing the flow of traffic, vehicle types, and more.

In retail, object detection can be employed for inventory management, tracking products on shelves, and even in checkout-free shopping experiences. Cameras equipped with object detection can track products that customers pick up and automatically charge them. Security systems employ object detection to identify unauthorized access, track individuals or vehicles, and recognize suspicious activities. It enhances the efficiency of surveillance by automating the monitoring process.

Farmers are leveraging object detection to identify and sort produce, detect diseases in crops, and even in automated harvesting. Drones equipped with cameras can provide aerial surveillance and detect areas that need attention. In manufacturing, object detection is utilized to identify defects in products, guide robotic arms, and automate sorting processes. It's crucial for quality control and increasing the efficiency of manufacturing lines.

In gaming and entertainment, object detection provides a basis for augmented reality experiences. It enables virtual objects to interact with real-world objects, enhancing user engagement. Object detection is used in monitoring wildlife, assessing the health of forests, and even in waste sorting. It provides valuable data to researchers and helps in conservation efforts.

For people with visual impairments, object detection can be utilized to describe the environment and assist in navigation, thus contributing to creating more accessible technologies. Object detection is an immensely versatile and powerful technique with a wide array of applications across various domains. Its integration into diverse fields has not only enhanced efficiency and accuracy but also fueled innovation and offered new possibilities. The continuous advancement in algorithms, computing power, and the availability of vast amounts of data ensures that object detection will remain at the forefront of technological evolution, finding new applications and enriching existing ones.

R-CNN (Region-based)

R-CNN, or Region-based Convolutional Neural Network, is a pioneering object detection algorithm that combines the power of convolutional neural networks (CNN) with region proposals to detect and classify objects in images. It was one of the first attempts to bring together the strengths of deep learning and region proposals for the task of object detection, paving the way for many advances in the field.

Following is a detailed look at the architecture and the functioning of R-CNN:

Generating Regions

R-CNN employs an external method to generate potential bounding boxes or regions where an object might be located. The most common technique used is Selective Search, which oversegments the image and merges similar regions, resulting in about 2000 region proposals.

Preprocessing

These region proposals are then warped to a fixed size so that they can be fed into a pre-trained CNN.

Feature Extraction

Each warped region proposal is passed through a pre-trained CNN (usually trained on ImageNet). This network extracts valuable features from each region, transforming them into a more compact and expressive representation. For example, the architecture might employ the well-known AlexNet.

Fully Connected Layers

The output from the convolutional layers is flattened and passed through one or more fully connected layers. This process helps in making the high-level abstractions more robust and suitable for classification.

Support Vector Machine (SVM)

On top of the CNN, R-CNN employs a set of binary Support Vector Machines (SVMs) to classify the regions into different object classes or background. There's an SVM for each class, trained to distinguish between that class and all the others.

Bounding Box Regression

Alongside the SVMs, a linear regression model is trained to refine the coordinates of the bounding boxes. This adjustment accounts for the discrepancies introduced during the region proposal and warping stages, making the final detection more accurate.

Computational Efficiency

One of the major limitations of R-CNN is its computational inefficiency. Since each region proposal is passed through the CNN, the feature extraction step becomes a bottleneck, especially when dealing with a large number of proposals.

Training Complexity

Training an R-CNN involves multiple stages, including pre-training the CNN, fine-tuning it for the object detection task, training the SVMs, and finally, the bounding box regressors. This multi-stage process can be intricate and time-consuming. R-CNN's architecture laid the foundation for subsequent advancements in object detection. Its successors, Fast R-CNN and Faster R-CNN, introduced novel components to address the challenges in R-CNN, improving efficiency without sacrificing accuracy.

Implement R-CNN Model: Object Detection

Implementing an R-CNN model is an engaging process that encompasses several steps, from preprocessing the image data to defining the model architecture and training. In the given below example, you will use the PASCAL VOC dataset, which is a well-known dataset in object detection, available here.

Preprocessing the Dataset

- Download and Unzip: Download the PASCAL VOC dataset and extract it into a suitable directory. The dataset is available in the following URL: http://host.robots.ox.ac.uk/pascal/VOC/databases.html

- Data Preparation: Preprocess the images and annotations, such as resizing and normalizing the images.

Region Proposals Generation

You can utilize Selective Search to generate region proposals. Libraries like OpenCV have built-in functions for this.

```
import cv2
ss = cv2.ximgproc.segmentation.createSelectiveSearchSegmentation()
ss.setBaseImage(image)
ss.switchToSelectiveSearchFast()
rects = ss.process()
```

CNN for Feature Extraction

Use a pre-trained CNN like VGG16 or AlexNet for feature extraction. In Python, you can utilize TensorFlow or Keras.

```
from tensorflow.keras.applications.vgg16 import VGG16

base_model = VGG16(weights='imagenet', include_top=False)
```

Training the Classifier (SVM)

- Preparing Data: Extract features for each region proposal using the CNN and prepare the labels using the ground truth data.

- Training the SVM: Use a library like scikit-learn to train a set of binary SVMs for each class.

```
from sklearn.svm import SVC

svm = SVC(kernel='linear')
svm.fit(features, labels)
```

Bounding Box Regression

- Model Definition: Define a simple linear regression model.

- Training: Train this model on the ground truth bounding boxes and the proposed regions.

```
from sklearn.linear_model import LinearRegression

regressor = LinearRegression()
regressor.fit(proposed_boxes, ground_truth_boxes)
```

Putting It All Together

- Pipeline Integration: Integrate all the above steps into a single pipeline.
- Testing the Model: Use your trained SVM and bounding box regressor to detect objects in the test images.

Your final code should follow a structure that:

1. Loads the data
2. Generates region proposals
3. Extracts features using a CNN
4. Trains SVM for classification
5. Trains regression for bounding box adjustment
6. Combines all steps for testing

Building an R-CNN from scratch is complex and might be outperformed by more recent architectures. Libraries like TensorFlow Object Detection API offer pre-built models that can be fine-tuned on your dataset, which might be a more efficient route for production-ready solutions. But implementing R-CNN by hand is an unparalleled educational experience that provides deep insights into how these models work.

YOLO Object Detection

YOLO (You Only Look Once) is another object detection architecture that has gained tremendous popularity for its speed and efficiency. Following is a detailed overview of YOLO, its architecture, and a comparison with R-CNN to showcase the differences.

YOLO Architecture

The main selling point of YOLO is that it looks at an image only once and predicts the bounding boxes and class labels simultaneously. It treats the object detection task as a single regression problem.

Grid Division

Image Division: The input image is divided into a grid (e.g., 13x13).
Object Assignment: Each grid cell predicts an object if the center of the object falls into it.

Bounding Boxes Prediction

Boxes per Cell: Each grid cell predicts multiple bounding boxes and their confidence scores. Confidence represents the IOU (Intersection Over Union) between the predicted box and any ground truth.

Class Prediction

Class Probabilities: Each grid cell also predicts a class probability distribution over predefined classes.

Loss Function

Combined Loss: The loss function combines coordinates loss, confidence loss, and class loss.

Final Predictions

Thresholding and Non-Max Suppression: Post-processing steps such as thresholding on confidence and non-max suppression are performed to get the final predictions.

Comparison with R-CNN

YOLO and R-CNN have fundamental differences in their approach to object detection.

Speed

YOLO: As the name suggests, YOLO performs object detection in one pass, making it significantly faster.
R-CNN: R-CNN involves multiple steps, including region proposals and feature extraction for each proposal, making it computationally expensive.

Detection Methodology

YOLO: Detects objects by dividing the entire image into a grid and making predictions for each cell.
R-CNN: Relies on region proposals and then classifies and adjusts each proposal.

Real-time Applications

YOLO: Suitable for real-time applications due to its speed.
R-CNN: Not typically used for real-time applications as it is slower.

Complexity
YOLO: The architecture is more unified and treats detection as a single problem.
R-CNN: More complex due to separate stages for proposals, feature extraction, and classification.

Performance
YOLO: Tends to have more localization errors compared to R-CNN but is usually good enough for many applications.
R-CNN: Can achieve higher accuracy but at the cost of speed and complexity.

Flexibility
YOLO: Less flexible in handling objects of various sizes due to grid division.
R-CNN: More flexible due to selective search for region proposals.

Versions of YOLO
YOLO has seen multiple versions, including YOLOv1, YOLOv2 (Darknet-19), YOLOv3, etc., each with improvements in various aspects.

Understanding both YOLO and R-CNN offers insights into the evolution of object detection. While R-CNN takes a more segmented approach to detection, YOLO simplifies the process into a single step. The choice between them can be dependent on the specific requirements of a project, such as the need for real-time detection or higher accuracy.

Sample Program: Implement YOLO Model

Environment Preparation

To kickstart the YOLO implementation, make sure you have TensorFlow and OpenCV installed on your system. These libraries are essential for neural network operations and image manipulation, respectively.

Dataset Utilization

You will continue to use the same open-source dataset that we explored in the previous sections. The steps for loading and preprocessing the dataset remain consistent, so you can refer back to earlier sections for guidance on this aspect.

Configuring the YOLO Model

YOLO has specific requirements when it comes to configuration and weight files. Navigate to the official YOLO website to download the weight and configuration files for YOLOv3 or any other version that aligns with your project needs.

Building the YOLO Model

You will leverage the pre-trained weights and write a script to build the model in TensorFlow.

```
import cv2
import numpy as np

# Load YOLO
net = cv2.dnn.readNet("yolov3.weights", "yolov3.cfg")
layer_names = net.getLayerNames()
output_layers = [layer_names[i[0] - 1] for i in net.getUnconnectedOutLayers()]

# Load classes
with open("coco.names", "r") as file:
    classes = [line.strip() for line in file.readlines()]
```

Preprocessing the Image

The image preprocessing steps include resizing, normalization, and reshaping, as YOLO requires specific input dimensions.

```
image = cv2.imread("image.jpg")
blob = cv2.dnn.blobFromImage(image, scalefactor=0.00392, size=(416, 416), mean=(0,
0, 0), swapRB=True, crop=False)
net.setInput(blob)
```

Running the Forward Pass

You will run the forward pass through the YOLO network to get the detected objects.

```
outs = net.forward(output_layers)
```

Processing the Outputs

YOLO returns several bounding boxes, confidence scores, and class IDs. You will process these to filter out the valid detections.

```
for out in outs:
    for detection in out:
        scores = detection[5:]
        class_id = np.argmax(scores)
        confidence = scores[class_id]

        if confidence > 0.5: # Threshold
            # Code to extract bounding box, draw on the image, etc.
```

Non-Maximum Suppression

This step helps in removing redundant bounding boxes by keeping only the ones with the highest confidence.

```
indices = cv2.dnn.NMSBoxes(boxes, confidences, 0.5, 0.4)
for i in indices:
    i = i[0]
    box = boxes[i]
    label = str(classes[class_ids[i]])
    confidence = confidences[i]
    color = colors[class_ids[i]]
    cv2.rectangle(image, (box[0], box[1]), (box[0] + box[2], box[1] + box[3]), color, 2)
```

Displaying the Results

You will use OpenCV to visualize the detected objects along with their bounding boxes.

```
cv2.imshow("Image", image)
cv2.waitKey(0)
cv2.destroyAllWindows()
```

These steps should provide you with a practical implementation of the YOLO model for object detection on the chosen dataset. Building upon this foundation, you can explore more advanced features, fine-tuning, or integration into larger systems.

Model Evaluation Metrics

Evaluation metrics play an essential role in assessing the performance of machine learning models, especially in object detection tasks like those demonstrated with R-CNN and YOLO. These metrics allow us to compare models, choose optimal parameters, and determine the model's effectiveness in detecting objects.

Common Evaluation Metrics for Object Detection

1. Precision: Precision calculates the number of true positives divided by the sum of true positives and false positives. It tells us the percentage of correctly identified positive detections.

2. Recall: Recall calculates the number of true positives divided by the sum of true positives and false negatives. It's a measure of the model's ability to detect all possible positives.

3. F1-Score: The F1-Score is the harmonic mean of precision and recall, providing a balance between these two metrics.

4. Intersection over Union (IoU): IoU measures the overlap between two boundaries. It's calculated by dividing the intersection of the predicted bounding box with the actual bounding box by their union. High IoU means the prediction is close to the ground truth.

5. Mean Average Precision (mAP): mAP is widely used in object detection. It calculates the average precision at different recall levels. It's a unified metric that takes into consideration different object classes and prediction thresholds.

6. ROC Curve and AUC: The Receiver Operating Characteristic curve plots the true positive rate against the false positive rate, and the Area Under the Curve (AUC) summarizes this curve into a single value, capturing the model's ability to discriminate between positive and negative classes.

Evaluating R-CNN and YOLO Models

Precision, Recall, and F1-Score

You can calculate these metrics using libraries like Scikit-Learn. Below is how you might do it:

```
from sklearn.metrics import precision_score, recall_score, f1_score

precision = precision_score(y_true, y_pred)
```

```
recall = recall_score(y_true, y_pred)
f1 = f1_score(y_true, y_pred)
```

Intersection over Union (IoU)

For object detection, you might calculate IoU as follows:

```
def iou(box1, box2):
    x1, y1, x2, y2 = box1
    x1g, y1g, x2g, y2g = box2

    xi1, yi1, xi2, yi2 = max(x1, x1g), max(y1, y1g), min(x2, x2g), min(y2, y2g)
    intersection_area = max(xi2 - xi1, 0) * max(yi2 - yi1, 0)
    box1_area = (x2 - x1) * (y2 - y1)
    box2_area = (x2g - x1g) * (y2g - y1g)

    union_area = box1_area + box2_area - intersection_area
    return intersection_area / union_area
```

True Positives, False Positives, and False Negatives

- True Positives (TP): These are correctly predicted positive values.
- False Positives (FP): These occur when the model incorrectly predicts a positive value.
- False Negatives (FN): These happen when the model incorrectly predicts a negative value.

These above basic concepts form the foundation for understanding the metrics discussed earlier, and they allow for more nuanced interpretations.

Sensitivity and Specificity

- Sensitivity: Also known as True Positive Rate or Recall. It quantifies the model's ability to detect all relevant instances.
- Specificity: Also known as the True Negative Rate. It measures the proportion of actual negatives that are correctly identified.

Confidence Thresholds

In object detection, confidence thresholds are used to determine what constitutes a detection.

Adjusting this threshold affects the balance between precision and recall, allowing for fine-tuning based on specific needs.

Average Precision (AP) at different IoU Thresholds

AP is calculated at various IoU thresholds to consider different degrees of overlap between the predicted and actual bounding boxes. This gives a more granular understanding of the model's performance.

Confusion Matrix

The confusion matrix gives a detailed view of how the model's predictions are distributed across different classes, allowing for the identification of specific weaknesses or biases in the model.

Harmonizing Precision and Recall

Precision-Recall curves can be used to understand the trade-off between precision and recall at different threshold levels.

Implementing Metrics in TensorFlow

TensorFlow provides built-in functions for many common metrics, which can be easily integrated into a training pipeline.

For example:

```
import tensorflow as tf

model.compile(optimizer='adam',
        loss='sparse_categorical_crossentropy',
        metrics=['accuracy', tf.keras.metrics.Precision(), tf.keras.metrics.Recall()])
```

No single metric can capture all aspects of a model's performance, so it's usually advisable to consider a combination of metrics. The choice of metrics should align with the business objectives or specific goals of the task. Understanding the potential biases in the data and the model's impact on different population groups may require careful consideration and possibly the development of specific fairness metrics.

Also, continuous monitoring and evaluation may be necessary in a production environment to detect drift and changes in the underlying data distribution.

Data Annotation

Overview

Data annotation is an essential aspect of data preparation for machine learning models, particularly in object detection tasks. Data annotation refers to the process of labeling or marking data, such as images, to provide ground-truth information that can be used to train, validate, and test machine learning models. In object detection tasks, this typically involves drawing bounding boxes around objects and assigning class labels.

Importance

- Quality Assurance: The accuracy of the annotated data directly impacts the model's performance.
- Customization: Enables the creation of datasets tailored to specific tasks or domains.
- Enables Supervised Learning: Provides the necessary ground truth that the model tries to predict during training.

Types of Annotation

- Bounding Boxes: Used in object detection to identify the location of an object within an image.
- Semantic Segmentation: Assigns a class label to each pixel in an image, providing a detailed understanding of the scene.
- Keypoint Annotation: Used to identify specific points of interest within an object, like human joints in pose estimation.

Various tools are available for manual annotation, including open-source options like RectLabel, Labelbox, and VGG Image Annotator (VIA).

Brief Steps for Annotating Data

- Select a Tool: Choose an annotation tool that fits your needs and the specific task.
- Load the Data: Import the images or data to be annotated.
- Define Classes: Set up the class labels that correspond to the objects you want to detect.
- Annotate: Draw bounding boxes around each object and assign the appropriate class label.

- Quality Control: Review the annotations for accuracy and consistency, making corrections as needed.
- Export: Save the annotated data in a format suitable for your machine learning framework (e.g., JSON, XML).

While manual annotation is common, there are also automated or semi-automated techniques that leverage existing models to speed up the process. For instance, pre-trained models can provide initial annotations that are then refined manually.

Using Annotated Data in TensorFlow

Once data is annotated, it can be used to train object detection models. Following is an example code snippet for loading annotated data into TensorFlow:

```
import tensorflow as tf

# Define the path to the annotated data
annotation_file = 'path/to/annotations.json'

# Load the data
with open(annotation_file, 'r') as file:
    annotations = json.load(file)

# Parse the data into a format suitable for training
def parse_annotation(annotations):
    # Parsing logic here
    return images, bounding_boxes, class_labels

# Create a dataset
images, bounding_boxes, class_labels = parse_annotation(annotations)
dataset = tf.data.Dataset.from_tensor_slices((images, bounding_boxes, class_labels))
```

Data annotation requires attention to detail, understanding of the task, and sometimes significant manual effort. However, it's an indispensable part of building robust object detection models. With careful selection of tools, adhering to best practices, and leveraging automation where appropriate, you can create high-quality annotated data that sets the foundation for successful modeling. Whether you're working with R-CNN, YOLO, or any other object detection architecture, proper data annotation is a critical step in machine learning or a deep learning pipeline.

Summary

In this chapter, we delved into object detection, exploring its many facets and methodologies. Beginning with an overview of object detection, we examined real-world applications and how this technology is being utilized across various industries. Understanding these applications set the stage for a comprehensive study of architectures like R-CNN and YOLO, each offering unique features and advantages.

We then shifted our focus to practical implementation, demonstrating how to build models using R-CNN and YOLO. These hands-on examples, coupled with an exploration of the open-source datasets, offered an invaluable guide for constructing object detection systems. We not only investigated the building of models but also the vital process of evaluating them through various metrics, understanding how to gauge the quality and performance of the models.

Data annotation became a highlight of the chapter as we dived deep into its conceptual framework and practical application. The process was laid out step-by-step, from selecting the right tool to the final export of annotated data, and understanding its significance in training quality object detection models. We also explored automation in data annotation, offering insights into efficient practices that can save time and resources.

The chapter rounded off with a practical approach to image data preparation, specifically data annotation. This detailed walkthrough provided a clear understanding of different annotation types, including bounding boxes, semantic segmentation, and keypoint annotation. We explored various tools, manual and automated methods, and their integration into TensorFlow. By studying this intricate process, you gain essential insights into the initial stages of model building, reinforcing the importance of accurate data annotation in the development of reliable and efficient object detection systems.

CHAPTER 6: TEXT RECOGNITION AND NATURAL LANGUAGE PROCESSING

Overview

Text recognition and Natural Language Processing (NLP) have emerged as transformative technologies that bridge the gap between human communication and computational understanding. In this chapter, you will explore the core concepts of these fields and how they are currently applied in various domains.

Text Recognition

Text recognition refers to the conversion of visual text data into machine-encoded text. It's not merely confined to reading printed or handwritten material; it encompasses a broader array of applications such as:

- Optical Character Recognition (OCR): OCR engines can digitize printed text from scanned documents, images, PDF files, and other digital formats into searchable and editable content. This allows processing of large volumes of documents rapidly.
- License Plate Recognition: Cameras combined with text recognition software enable automatic reading of license plates on vehicles for applications like electronic toll collection, law enforcement, and intelligent transportation systems.
- Bank Check Processing: Banks use text recognition to streamline processing and digitization of checks by automatically extracting handwritten and printed text like names, amounts, account numbers etc.
- Scene Text Recognition: This involves detecting and recognizing text found in real-world scenes like signboards, product packaging, banners, and more in images and video. Useful for augmented reality applications.
- Handwriting Recognition: Digital pen technology and handwriting recognition algorithms convert handwritten input from devices like tablets and styluses into standard text. Useful for note-taking and data entry.
- Document Digitization: Libraries, archives, and offices use text recognition on collections of historical handwritten or printed documents to create searchable digital copies for better storage and retrieval.
- Invoice Processing: Text recognition automates the extraction of key information like item descriptions, quantities, totals, addresses etc. from invoice documents.

Natural Language Processing (NLP)

Natural Language Processing is a field at the intersection of computer science, artificial intelligence, and linguistics. Its goal is to enable computers to understand, interpret, generate, and respond to human languages in a valuable way. Following is how NLP is being utilized in various industries:

- Customer Service Bots: NLP-powered chatbots are providing 24/7 customer service, handling inquiries, and even processing orders.
- Sentiment Analysis: Companies are using NLP to gauge consumer sentiment from social

media, reviews, and other online sources.

- Speech Recognition: Voice assistants like Siri and Alexa use NLP to understand and respond to user commands.
- Machine Translation: NLP is behind the ability of platforms like Google Translate to convert text or speech from one language to another.
- Healthcare: In healthcare, NLP is used for tasks such as converting voice notes into structured data, enabling more streamlined patient care.

Text Recognition and NLP: Convergence

The convergence of text recognition and NLP enables many innovative applications:

- Document Automation: OCR and NLP integrate to parse documents, extracting structured data and interpreting content to auto-fill forms, route invoices, or retrieve information. This brings major efficiency gains to handling large volumes of documents in offices.
- Educational Tools: Text recognition can scan textbooks and convert them to alternate formats like audio books or different languages through translation. This assists students with visual impairments or language barriers in accessing educational materials.
- Legal and Compliance: Automated review of legal contracts by applying NLP techniques like named entity recognition and sentiment analysis on top of digitized documents extracted via text recognition. This also applies to regulatory compliance checks.
- Medical Documentation: Text recognition can digitize handwritten doctor notes and prescriptions coupled with NLP to automatically populate medical records or flag medication interactions.
- Customer Service: Call center systems can leverage text and speech recognition to analyze customer inquiries and documents like account statements to quickly provide personalized resolutions.
- Search and Recommendation: OCR allows converting menus, brochures, catalogs into structured data to power restaurant or travel recommendation systems based on customer preferences.

The above examples only scratch the surface of the vast and continually evolving landscape of text recognition and NLP. These technologies are fundamentally changing the way we interact with information and each other, driving efficiencies, and creating new opportunities across diverse sectors. The following sections of this chapter will delve deeper into the methodologies, algorithms, and practical implementations that power these compelling applications.

Text Preprocessing Process

Text preprocessing is a crucial step in Natural Language Processing (NLP) that prepares and cleans the text data for analysis and modeling. When working with TensorFlow, this process becomes streamlined and efficient. In this section, you will explore the process of text preprocessing using TensorFlow without diving into specific methods and techniques.

Text preprocessing is the process of converting raw text into a format that can be easily analyzed. In real-world data, text often comes in various forms and may include inconsistencies, such as different encodings, languages, or typos. Preprocessing aims to standardize this data to make it suitable for analysis.

TensorFlow provides a set of tools and libraries to assist in the preprocessing of text data. Following is a broad overview of the process:

Loading the Text Data

You'll start by importing the necessary libraries and loading the text data into a suitable data structure. TensorFlow provides functions to easily load data from various sources, such as files, URLs, or databases.

Tokenization

Tokenization is the process of splitting the text into smaller parts called tokens, usually words or subwords. TensorFlow offers tokenization methods through the TextVectorization layer or specialized tokenization libraries like Tokenizer.

Normalization

Text data often contains variations in letter casing, punctuation, or special characters. Normalization helps in converting text into a consistent form, such as converting all characters to lowercase. With TensorFlow, this can be achieved using pre defined normalization functions.

Text Encoding

After tokenization and normalization, the text data is typically encoded into numerical format. This conversion is necessary because machine learning models work with numerical values. TensorFlow provides various encoding techniques, such as one-hot encoding or embedding layers, to achieve this.

Sequencing and Padding

Text data often comes in varying lengths, and machine learning models require inputs of the same size. Sequencing and padding ensure that all text sequences are of the same length. TensorFlow provides functions like pad_sequences to handle this task efficiently.

Integration with Models

Once preprocessed, the text data can be fed into deep learning models for various NLP tasks like classification, translation, or summarization. TensorFlow's robust and flexible architecture ensures seamless integration with different types of models.

The above generalized steps provide a general framework for text preprocessing in TensorFlow. By using these tools and libraries, you can transform raw text data into a format that is ready for modeling. In subsequent sections, you will dive deeper into each of these stages and explore the specific methods and techniques used in text preprocessing.

Text Preprocessing and Cleaning Techniques

Text preprocessing is a vital stage in Natural Language Processing (NLP), and several techniques and methods are employed to prepare text data for modeling. Below, you will explore these techniques in detail.

Tokenization

Tokenization is the process of breaking down a text into smaller units, such as words or subwords. It is one of the foundational techniques in text preprocessing.

Word Tokenization: It splits a text into individual words. This is common in languages with space-separated words.
Subword Tokenization: In some languages, it's beneficial to split text into smaller units like syllables or even individual characters.
Sentence Tokenization: This breaks a text into individual sentences, which can be useful in tasks like sentiment analysis or translation.

Text Normalization

The primary goal of text normalization is to transform the text into a uniform format, making it easier to analyze. This involves several key techniques:

1. Lowercasing: Transforming all text characters to lowercase ensures uniformity and makes the text case-insensitive, facilitating easier text matching.

2. Stemming: This technique trims off the prefixes or suffixes from words to obtain their root form. For example, "running" becomes "run." This is particularly useful for reducing the dimensionality of the text data.

3. Lemmatization: Unlike stemming, lemmatization takes into account the meaning of the word and transforms it into its base or dictionary form. For instance, "went" becomes "go."

4. Elimination of Punctuation and Special Characters: Punctuation marks and special characters often don't contribute to the semantic meaning of text and are usually removed during preprocessing.

Text Encoding

Machine learning models require numerical input, necessitating the conversion of text data into a numerical format. The given below are some commonly used methods:

1. One-Hot Encoding: In this approach, each unique word in the vocabulary is represented as a binary vector. Only one element in the vector is "hot" (marked as 1), while the rest are zeros. This is a straightforward but often memory-intensive method.

2. Word Embedding: A more advanced technique, word embedding represents words in a dense vector space where the vector positions capture semantic relationships between words. Popular algorithms for word embedding include Word2Vec and GloVe.

Handling Stop Words

Stop words like "and," "or," "the," and "is" usually don't carry significant semantic meaning and are often removed during text preprocessing. There are two primary ways to handle stop words:

1. Utilizing Predefined Lists: Various Natural Language Processing (NLP) libraries offer predefined lists of stop words that can be readily used for removal.

2. Custom Stop Word Removal: Depending on the specific requirements of your project, you may need to define a custom list of stop words for removal. This allows for greater flexibility and can be tailored to suit the nuances of the text data you are working with.

Text Sequencing and Padding

Text Sequencing and Padding for Uniformity:

1. Sequencing Text Data: In natural language processing tasks, text data often comes in varying lengths. To standardize this, text is usually converted into sequences of tokens or words. This transformation is known as text sequencing.

2. Padding for Consistency: After sequencing, you may still have sequences of different lengths. Padding is the process of filling short sequences with zeros or other specified values to make all sequences uniform in length. This ensures that the neural network receives input of consistent size.

Handling Missing Values

Missing or null values in the text data must be handled to avoid errors in analysis. Strategies for Handling Missing or Null Values are:

1. Eliminating Missing Values: One straightforward approach to deal with missing or null values is to remove the entire rows or columns where these values are found. This is often the quickest way to ensure data integrity but may result in loss of valuable data.

2. Imputation Techniques: Alternatively, missing values can be replaced using statistical methods like mean, median, or mode imputation. You can also use predefined constants to fill in these gaps, depending on the nature of your dataset and the problem you are trying to solve.

Text Augmentation

Text augmentation expands the dataset by creating variations of the existing text. Following are the techniques:

1. Synonym Substitution: One common text augmentation technique is to replace words in the text with their synonyms. This adds variability to the dataset while preserving the original meaning.

2. Back-and-Forth Translation: Another innovative method is back translation. Here, the text is first translated into a different language and then translated back into the original language. This often results in slight variations that can enrich the dataset.

3. Random Deletion and Insertion: To further augment the text, you can randomly delete words from sentences or insert new words at random positions. This introduces more diversity into the dataset, making the model more robust.

N-grams

N-grams are sequences of 'n' contiguous items extracted from a given sample of text. They are highly useful for capturing the inherent patterns and structures within the text. For example, bigrams (2-grams) capture two-word combinations, trigrams (3-grams) capture three-word combinations, and so on. Utilizing N-grams can significantly improve the performance of text classification and sentiment analysis tasks.

By combining and customizing these techniques, practitioners can prepare and clean their text data for a wide variety of NLP tasks. Understanding the nature of the data and the requirements of the specific task will walkthrough the choice of techniques to use. The flexibility and adaptability of these methods are key factors in the success of modern NLP.

Sample Program: Perform Text Preprocessing

Text preprocessing and cleaning are crucial for building robust NLP models. Below, you will walk through the practical process of performing text preprocessing and cleaning using TensorFlow. For this demonstration, you will be using the IMDb movie review dataset available in the TensorFlow datasets package.

Importing Libraries and Loading Dataset

First, let us import the necessary libraries and load the IMDb dataset.

```
import tensorflow as tf
import tensorflow_datasets as tfds
from tensorflow.keras.preprocessing.text import Tokenizer
from tensorflow.keras.preprocessing.sequence import pad_sequences

# Load the IMDb dataset
(train_data, test_data), info = tfds.load(
    'imdb_reviews',
    split=['train', 'test'],
    with_info=True,
    as_supervised=True
)
```

You can find more information about the dataset in the following URL:
https://www.tensorflow.org/datasets/catalog/imdb_reviews

Tokenization

Let us tokenize the text data. Tokenization splits the text into individual words or tokens.

```
tokenizer = Tokenizer(num_words=10000, oov_token="<OOV>")
train_texts = [text.numpy().decode('utf-8') for text, label in train_data]
tokenizer.fit_on_texts(train_texts)
```

Text Sequencing

Converting the text into sequences of numbers.

```
train_sequences = tokenizer.texts_to_sequences(train_texts)
```

Padding

To ensure that the sequences have the same length, we can pad shorter sequences.

```
padded_train_sequences = pad_sequences(train_sequences, maxlen=200,
padding='post')
```

Text Normalization

Text normalization includes techniques like lowercasing. This is usually handled during tokenization in the Tokenizer class in the earlier steps discussed..

Handling Stop Words

You can handle stop words during tokenization by configuring the Tokenizer.

```
from tensorflow.keras.preprocessing.text import text_to_word_sequence

# Define stop words
stop_words = ["the", "and", "is", "of"]

# Function to remove stop words
def remove_stop_words(text):
    words = text_to_word_sequence(text)
    return " ".join([word for word in words if word not in stop_words])

# Apply to training texts
train_texts = [remove_stop_words(text) for text in train_texts]
```

Text Encoding

If you wish to use word embeddings, you can include an embedding layer in your model.

```
model = tf.keras.Sequential([
```

```
    tf.keras.layers.Embedding(10000, 16, input_length=200),
    # Additional layers
])
```

The above demonstration includes tokenization, sequencing, padding, normalization, stop word removal, and optional steps like text encoding. These techniques are essential for preparing text data for various NLP tasks, and TensorFlow provides a comprehensive toolkit for performing these operations efficiently and effectively.

Influence of LSTM for NLP

Long Short-Term Memory (LSTM) networks, a specific type of recurrent neural network (RNN), have gained immense popularity in the field of Natural Language Processing (NLP). Their unique architecture enables them to capture sequential information and long-term dependencies, making them suitable for various NLP tasks.

Following is a detailed examination of the potential and power of LSTM for NLP:

Handling Sequential Data

Unlike traditional feed-forward neural networks, LSTM networks maintain a hidden state across the sequence, allowing them to carry information along as they process each element in a series. In NLP, this sequence is typically a sentence or document, and understanding the order of words is crucial for tasks like sentiment analysis, translation, and speech recognition.

Overcoming the Vanishing Gradient Problem

Standard RNNs are challenged by the vanishing gradient problem, which makes it difficult for the network to learn and leverage long-term dependencies in the data. LSTM's unique gating mechanism, with forget, input, and output gates, helps manage the flow of information through the network, ensuring that essential long-term patterns are retained and unnecessary information is forgotten. This structure makes them particularly well-suited for understanding the contextual relationships between words in a sentence, even over long distances.

Versatility in NLP Applications

LSTM's ability to capture sequential dependencies has paved the way for its success in a wide array of NLP applications.

For instance:

1. Machine Translation: LSTMs are used to understand the sequential nature of sentences in

one language and translate them into another.
2. Speech Recognition: They can process audio data over time, recognizing patterns in spoken language.
3. Text Generation: LSTMs have been employed in generating human-like text, capturing the intricacies of language structure.
4. Sentiment Analysis: By understanding the context and order of words, LSTMs can gauge the underlying sentiment of a text fragment.

Bidirectional LSTMs

Bidirectional LSTMs (Bi-LSTMs) are an extension where two LSTM layers are used, one processing the sequence from start to end, and the other from end to start. This two-way analysis helps the network to capture context from both directions, offering a more comprehensive understanding of the sequence. In tasks like named entity recognition or part-of-speech tagging, this can provide significant improvements.

Integration with Other Neural Network Architectures

LSTMs can be seamlessly integrated with other neural network architectures like Convolutional Neural Networks (CNNs) to create hybrid models. For instance, CNNs can be used for feature extraction, and LSTMs for sequence modeling. This collaboration enhances the model's capability to recognize complex patterns and relationships within the data.

Support for Attention Mechanisms

Attention mechanisms, when combined with LSTMs, enable the model to focus on specific parts of the sequence when making predictions. This focus or 'attention' is dynamically determined during training. In tasks like machine translation, attention helps the model to align words and phrases in the source and target languages, mimicking the way humans translate between languages.

LSTM's strength in handling sequential data, overcoming the vanishing gradient problem, versatility in applications, capability to be bidirectional, integration with other architectures, and support for attention mechanisms makes it a powerful tool in the NLP domain. Its profound impact on understanding and generating human language has revolutionized many areas, from personal assistants to automated customer support systems.

Sample Program: LSTM-based Text Classifier

Utilizing Long Short-Term Memory (LSTM) networks for text classification is a powerful approach, capable of capturing the underlying nuances and sequential nature of textual data. In this demonstration, you will build an LSTM model to classify text using the TensorFlow library. You will use the IMDb dataset, a well-known collection of movie reviews labeled as positive or negative, available in TensorFlow's datasets as used previously.

Import Necessary Libraries

```
import tensorflow as tf
from tensorflow.keras.preprocessing.sequence import pad_sequences
from tensorflow.keras.layers import Embedding, LSTM, Dense
from tensorflow.keras.preprocessing.text import Tokenizer
from tensorflow.keras.models import Sequential
from tensorflow.keras.datasets import imdb
```

Load and Prepare the Dataset

Load the IMDb dataset, and then split it into training and testing sets.

```
(x_train, y_train), (x_test, y_test) = imdb.load_data(num_words=5000) # Limiting to
5000 most frequent words
```

Here, num_words=5000 keeps the 5000 most frequently occurring words in the training data.

Next, pad the sequences to the same length.

```
x_train = pad_sequences(x_train, maxlen=500)
x_test = pad_sequences(x_test, maxlen=500)
```

We are truncating or padding the sequences to a length of 500 for uniformity.

Build the LSTM Model

Let us construct the LSTM model with an embedding layer.

```
model = Sequential()
model.add(Embedding(input_dim=5000, output_dim=32, input_length=500))
model.add(LSTM(100))
model.add(Dense(1, activation='sigmoid'))
```

```
model.compile(loss='binary_crossentropy', optimizer='adam', metrics=['accuracy'])
```

In the above,:

- Embedding Layer: Transforms the integer-encoded vocabulary into dense vectors of fixed size, here 32. It's connected to the input layer, which receives the input sequences.
- LSTM Layer: With 100 memory units, manages the sequence input.
- Dense Layer: Outputs the final classification prediction, using the sigmoid activation function for binary classification.

Train the LSTM Model

Now you will train our model on the training data.

```
model.fit(x_train, y_train, validation_data=(x_test, y_test), epochs=3, batch_size=64)
```

You can adjust the number of epochs and batch size as needed.

Evaluate the Model

Finally, evaluate the model on the test set to understand its performance.

```
loss, accuracy = model.evaluate(x_test, y_test)
print("Test Accuracy: {:.2f}%".format(accuracy * 100))
```

This code prints the model's accuracy on the test data.

Make Predictions

You can now use the trained LSTM model to classify new reviews.

```
# Example of a new review
new_review = "The movie was fantastic! Highly recommend watching."
# Preprocess and tokenize as done with training data
# Predict using the model
prediction = model.predict(new_preprocessed_review)
```

This method of utilizing LSTM for text classification captures the sequential relationships in the text, which enables an understanding of context and sentiment that may be missed by more simplistic models. The ability to train such a model on custom datasets for various classification tasks, such as sentiment analysis or topic categorization, demonstrates the versatility and effectiveness of LSTMs in the domain of text processing and Natural Language Processing.

Neural Network-based Sentiment Analysis

Sentiment Analysis is a Natural Language Processing (NLP) technique used to determine the sentiment or emotion expressed in a piece of text. It has applications ranging from understanding customer reviews to social media monitoring. Neural network-based sentiment analysis builds upon deep learning architectures like Convolutional Neural Networks (CNN) or Recurrent Neural Networks (RNN) like LSTM. In this section, you will explore the process of neural network-based sentiment analysis and follow it with a practical example using the IMDb dataset.

Neural Network-Based Sentiment Analysis Process

Data Collection and Preprocessing

Collecting a dataset that contains text along with sentiment labels is the first step. The IMDb dataset is a perfect example, with movie reviews labeled as positive or negative. Preprocessing the data involves tokenization, padding, and encoding. This converts the raw text into a numerical format suitable for input into a neural network.

Model Selection

Depending on the nature of the data, an appropriate neural network architecture is chosen. Common choices include CNNs for capturing local patterns or RNNs like LSTM for capturing sequential information.

Model Training

The selected model is trained using the preprocessed text data. During training, the model learns to associate textual features with the corresponding sentiment labels.

Model Evaluation

After training, the model's performance is evaluated using metrics like accuracy, precision, recall, or F1 score. Evaluation on a separate validation or test set ensures the robustness of the model.

Prediction

The trained model can now be used to predict the sentiment of unseen text.

Practical Implementation: IMDb Dataset Sentiment Analysis

Let us implement a sentiment analysis model using an LSTM neural network, leveraging the IMDb dataset.

Import Libraries

```
import tensorflow as tf
from tensorflow.keras.datasets import imdb
from tensorflow.keras.preprocessing.sequence import pad_sequences
from tensorflow.keras.models import Sequential
from tensorflow.keras.layers import Embedding, LSTM, Dense
```

Load and Prepare the Dataset
Load the IMDb dataset, and preprocess as previously discussed:

```
(x_train, y_train), (x_test, y_test) = imdb.load_data(num_words=5000)
x_train = pad_sequences(x_train, maxlen=500)
x_test = pad_sequences(x_test, maxlen=500)
```

Build the LSTM Model

```
model = Sequential()
model.add(Embedding(input_dim=5000, output_dim=32, input_length=500))
model.add(LSTM(100))
model.add(Dense(1, activation='sigmoid'))

model.compile(loss='binary_crossentropy', optimizer='adam', metrics=['accuracy'])
```

Train the Model

```
model.fit(x_train, y_train, validation_data=(x_test, y_test), epochs=3, batch_size=64)
```

Evaluate and Make Predictions

```
loss, accuracy = model.evaluate(x_test, y_test)
print("Test Accuracy: {:.2f}%".format(accuracy * 100))
```

You can use this trained model to predict the sentiment of any given text input. The process discussed above is not only applicable to sentiment analysis but can be adapted for other text classification tasks as well, demonstrating the versatility of neural network-based models in the field of NLP.

Seq2Seq Models

Seq2Seq, or Sequence-to-Sequence models, are a class of deep learning models specifically designed to handle sequences. They're extensively used in various NLP tasks such as machine translation, text summarization, speech recognition, and more.

Let us dive into a comprehensive understanding of the architecture, functionality, and usage of seq2seq models.

Seq2Seq Architecture

Encoder

The encoder's job is to process the input sequence and compress this information into a context vector, often the final hidden state of the encoder RNN. It essentially captures the entire information of the input sequence.

- Input Sequence: This could be a sequence of words, characters, or even phonemes, depending on the application.
- RNN Layers: Typically, RNNs like LSTM or GRU are used to process the sequence. These networks are excellent at handling sequential data, capturing the temporal dependencies within the sequence.
- Context Vector: The final hidden state of the encoder RNN acts as the context vector that encapsulates the entire information of the input sequence.

Decoder

The decoder takes the context vector and translates it into the output sequence, one element at a time. It essentially decodes the information contained in the context vector into a different sequence.

- Initial State: The context vector acts as the initial hidden state for the decoder RNN.
- RNN Layers: Similar to the encoder, the decoder also utilizes RNN layers like LSTM or GRU to generate the output sequence.
- Output Sequence: The decoder generates the output sequence step-by-step, using its previous predictions as inputs for subsequent steps.

Applications of Seq2Seq Models

- Machine Translation: Translating text from one language to another. The input sequence is the text in the source language, and the output sequence is the translation in the target language.

- Text Summarization: Condensing a longer text into a short summary. The original text is processed by the encoder, and the decoder generates the summary.
- Speech Recognition: Converting spoken language into text. The input sequence could be a waveform or spectrogram, and the output sequence is the corresponding text.
- Image Captioning: Generating a textual description of an image. The encoder can be a CNN that processes the image, and the decoder is an RNN that generates the caption.
- Chatbots and Conversational Agents: Generating responses in a conversation. The input sequence is the conversation history, and the output sequence is the chatbot's response.

To sum up, seq2seq models represent a versatile and powerful class of deep learning models for sequence-based tasks. By understanding the intricate interplay between the encoder and decoder, the architecture can be adapted and customized for a wide array of applications, ranging from language translation to speech synthesis, contributing immensely to the advancement of machine learning and artificial intelligence.

Sample Program: Seq2Seq Model for Language Translation

Building a Sequence-to-Sequence (seq2seq) model for language translation can be broken down into the following stages:

Data Preparation

Download Dataset

You can use the English-to-German translation dataset available in many open-source libraries. For example, the IWSLT dataset is widely used.

Dataset URL: https://pytorch.org/text/stable/datasets.html#iwslt2016

Preprocessing Text Data

Preprocessing includes tasks like tokenizing the text into words, converting words to integers, and padding sequences so that they are the same length.

```
from tensorflow.keras.preprocessing.text import Tokenizer
from tensorflow.keras.preprocessing.sequence import pad_sequences

def tokenize_and_pad(texts, max_len):
```

```
    tokenizer = Tokenizer()
    tokenizer.fit_on_texts(texts)
    sequences = tokenizer.texts_to_sequences(texts)
    padded_sequences = pad_sequences(sequences, maxlen=max_len, padding='post')
    return padded_sequences, tokenizer
```

Building the Seq2Seq Model

Encoder

The encoder takes the input sequence and compresses it into a context vector. You will use an LSTM layer for this.

```
from tensorflow.keras.layers import Input, LSTM, Embedding
from tensorflow.keras.models import Model

def build_encoder(input_dim, emb_dim, hidden_units):
    encoder_inputs = Input(shape=(None,))
    encoder_embedding = Embedding(input_dim, emb_dim)(encoder_inputs)
    encoder_lstm = LSTM(hidden_units, return_state=True)
    _, state_h, state_c = encoder_lstm(encoder_embedding)
    encoder_states = [state_h, state_c]
    return Model(encoder_inputs, encoder_states)
```

Decoder

The decoder takes the context vector from the encoder and produces the output sequence.

```
from tensorflow.keras.layers import LSTM, Dense

def build_decoder(input_dim, emb_dim, hidden_units):
    decoder_inputs = Input(shape=(None,))
    decoder_embedding = Embedding(input_dim, emb_dim)(decoder_inputs)
    decoder_lstm = LSTM(hidden_units, return_sequences=True, return_state=True)
    decoder_lstm_outputs, _, _ = decoder_lstm(decoder_embedding,
initial_state=encoder_states)
    decoder_dense = Dense(output_dim, activation='softmax')
```

```
    decoder_outputs = decoder_dense(decoder_lstm_outputs)
    return Model([decoder_inputs] + encoder_states, [decoder_outputs] +
decoder_states)
```

Training the Model

Compile the Model

```
model = Model([encoder_inputs, decoder_inputs], decoder_outputs)
model.compile(optimizer='rmsprop', loss='categorical_crossentropy')
```

Prepare Training Data

Tokenize and pad both the input sequences (English) and the target sequences (German).

Train the Model

```
model.fit([encoder_input_data, decoder_input_data], decoder_target_data,
batch_size=64, epochs=100)
```

Making Predictions

To translate new sentences, you'll need to define an inference model using the trained encoder and decoder.

```
# Inference Encoder
encoder_model = Model(encoder_inputs, encoder_states)

# Inference Decoder
decoder_state_input_h = Input(shape=(hidden_units,))
decoder_state_input_c = Input(shape=(hidden_units,))
decoder_states_inputs = [decoder_state_input_h, decoder_state_input_c]
decoder_lstm_outputs, state_h, state_c = decoder_lstm(decoder_embedding,
initial_state=decoder_states_inputs)
decoder_states = [state_h, state_c]
decoder_outputs = decoder_dense(decoder_lstm_outputs)
```

```
decoder_model = Model([decoder_inputs] + decoder_states_inputs, [decoder_outputs]
+ decoder_states)
```

Navigating through the world of inference models, you now have the capability to encode an input sequence and subsequently decode the generated context vector into a translated output. This practical walkthrough, although a brief example offers an in-depth exploration into constructing a sequence-to-sequence (seq2seq) model specifically designed for language translation. As you delve into the intricacies of the architecture and engage in a step-by-step implementation, you'll gain the expertise needed to experiment, optimize, and deploy this robust deep learning methodology for your own language translation projects.

Summary

In this chapter, we embarked on an in-depth exploration of text recognition and natural language processing (NLP), focusing on various techniques, models, and practical implementations. We started by understanding the significance of text preprocessing, including cleaning, tokenizing, and handling different encodings. The techniques covered were essential for preparing data for NLP tasks, ensuring that the input data is consistent and appropriate for further analysis.

Moving ahead, we delved into Long Short-Term Memory (LSTM) networks, showcasing their potential in handling sequential data. Practical examples guided us through building LSTM models for text classification, providing insights into this powerful recurrent neural network architecture. We further extended our knowledge to sentiment analysis, learning how neural networks can gauge emotions or opinions from textual data.

The chapter also introduced sequence-to-sequence (seq2seq) models, concentrating on their use in language translation tasks. Through hands-on examples, we explored how seq2seq models function, translating text from one language to another. We experimented with these models, gaining insights into their architecture, training, and real-world applications.

CHAPTER 7: STRATEGIES TO PREVENT OVERFITTING

Overfitting and Underfitting: Overview

Overfitting and underfitting are crucial concepts in machine learning and deep learning, fundamentally shaping the way models generalize from the data they are trained on. Understanding these phenomena is essential for developing models that are capable of making accurate predictions on unseen data.

Overfitting

Overfitting occurs when a model is trained too well on the training data, capturing even the noise and random fluctuations in the data. While this leads to an impressive performance on the training set, it hampers the model's ability to generalize to unseen or validation data. Essentially, an overfitted model has learned the training data too well, including its peculiarities and outliers, making it less effective in handling new, unseen examples.

Reasons for overfitting can include too complex a model for the given data, lack of regularization, or insufficient training data. Techniques to combat overfitting include regularization (such as L1 or L2 regularization), early stopping, pruning, dropout, or using more data.

Underfitting

Underfitting, on the other hand, is the opposite problem. It occurs when a model is too simple to capture the underlying patterns and relationships in the data. An underfitted model performs poorly not only on unseen data but also on the training set itself. This is usually a sign that the model lacks the complexity or capacity to understand the data.

Reasons for underfitting can include too simple a model architecture, too much regularization, or improper feature selection. Resolving underfitting may require increasing the model's complexity, reducing regularization, or using feature engineering to better represent the data.

Balancing Overfitting and Underfitting

Striking the right balance between overfitting and underfitting is a delicate and crucial task in model development. A model that is too complex risks overfitting, learning the noise rather than the signal. Conversely, a model that is too simple may fail to capture essential information, leading to underfitting.

Model validation techniques, such as cross-validation, help in assessing how well the model generalizes from the training data. Train-validation-test splits, learning curves, and model comparison with different complexities are tools that can be employed to find the right balance.

In deep learning, with models that often have a large number of parameters, the risk of overfitting is particularly high. Regularization techniques, proper validation, and a thoughtful approach to model selection and architecture design are vital.

Just to summarize, understanding overfitting and underfitting, their causes, symptoms, and strategies to combat them, is fundamental to creating models that can generalize well from the data they are trained on. This understanding guides the choice of model, the training process, and the evaluation strategy, shaping the success of the machine learning or deep learning application.

Regularization Techniques

Regularization is a set of techniques used to prevent overfitting in machine learning and deep learning models. It does this by adding some form of penalty to the loss function, constraining the model and discouraging it from fitting to the high noise in the training data.

Let us dive deeper into some common regularization techniques, demonstrating them with examples.

L1 Regularization (Lasso)

L1 regularization adds the sum of the absolute values of the weights as a penalty to the loss function. It's known as "Lasso" in linear regression context.

Equation:

$$\text{Loss} = \text{Original Loss} + \lambda \sum |w_i|$$

Example in Linear Regression using Scikit-Learn:

```
from sklearn.linear_model import Lasso

lasso_reg = Lasso(alpha=0.1)
lasso_reg.fit(X_train, y_train)
```

L2 Regularization (Ridge)

L2 regularization adds the sum of the squares of the weights as a penalty. It's commonly referred to as "Ridge" regression in linear models.

Equation:

$$\text{Loss} = \text{Original Loss} + \lambda \sum w_i^2$$

Example in Linear Regression using Scikit-Learn:

```
from sklearn.linear_model import Ridge

ridge_reg = Ridge(alpha=0.1)
ridge_reg.fit(X_train, y_train)
```

Elastic Net

Elastic Net combines L1 and L2 regularization, allowing for control over how much of each type of regularization to apply.

Equation:

$$\text{Loss} = \text{Original Loss} + \lambda_1 \sum |w_i| + \lambda_2 \sum w_i^2$$

Example using Scikit-Learn:

```
from sklearn.linear_model import ElasticNet

elastic_net = ElasticNet(alpha=0.1, l1_ratio=0.5)
elastic_net.fit(X_train, y_train)
```

Dropout

Dropout is a regularization technique specific to neural networks. During training, it randomly sets a fraction of the input units to 0 at each update, helping to prevent overfitting.

Example in TensorFlow:

```
import tensorflow as tf

model = tf.keras.models.Sequential([
    tf.keras.layers.Dense(64, activation='relu'),
    tf.keras.layers.Dropout(0.5),
    tf.keras.layers.Dense(1)
])
```

Early Stopping

Early stopping is a form of regularization used in training neural networks. It involves monitoring the validation loss and stopping training once the validation loss stops improving.

Example in TensorFlow:

```
early_stopping = tf.keras.callbacks.EarlyStopping(patience=2)
model.fit(X_train, y_train, validation_data=(X_val, y_val), callbacks=[early_stopping])
```

Batch Normalization

Though primarily a technique to help with training speed and stability, batch normalization can have a regularizing effect. It normalizes the output of a previous activation layer by subtracting the batch mean and dividing by the batch standard deviation.

Example in TensorFlow:

```
model.add(tf.keras.layers.BatchNormalization())
```

These regularization techniques can be combined and finely tuned to fit the specific needs of a given problem. By incorporating these methods into the model's architecture and training process, it's possible to reduce overfitting, making the model more robust and improving its ability to generalize from the training data to unseen examples. Regularization is a powerful tool in the machine learning toolkit, offering multiple avenues to control and guide the learning process.

Applying Regularization to LSTM

Let us apply some of the regularization techniques to the previously discussed LSTM model for text classification. This will allow us to see the practical implementation of regularization in a deep learning context, using TensorFlow as our framework.

Dataset Preparation

You will use the same dataset as before for text classification. Assuming we've already preprocessed the text data, let us quickly set up the training, validation, and test sets.

```
from sklearn.model_selection import train_test_split

X_train, X_val, y_train, y_val = train_test_split(X, y, test_size=0.2)
X_val, X_test, y_val, y_test = train_test_split(X_val, y_val, test_size=0.5)
```

Building the LSTM Model with Regularization

L1/L2 Regularization

In TensorFlow, L1 and L2 regularization can be applied directly to the weights of layers using tf.keras.regularizers.l1 and tf.keras.regularizers.l2.

```
from tensorflow.keras import regularizers

model = tf.keras.Sequential([
    tf.keras.layers.Embedding(input_dim=vocab_size, output_dim–64),
    tf.keras.layers.LSTM(64, kernel_regularizer=regularizers.l2(0.01)),
    tf.keras.layers.Dense(1, activation='sigmoid')
])
```

Dropout

Dropout can be applied between layers to prevent overfitting.

```
model = tf.keras.Sequential([
    tf.keras.layers.Embedding(input_dim=vocab_size, output_dim=64),
    tf.keras.layers.LSTM(64),
    tf.keras.layers.Dropout(0.5),
    tf.keras.layers.Dense(1, activation='sigmoid')
])
```

Early Stopping

Early stopping can be implemented as a callback during training.

```
early_stopping = tf.keras.callbacks.EarlyStopping(patience=2)

model.fit(X_train, y_train, validation_data=(X_val, y_val), epochs=10,
callbacks=[early_stopping])
```

Batch Normalization

Batch normalization can be applied between layers as well.

```
model = tf.keras.Sequential([
    tf.keras.layers.Embedding(input_dim=vocab_size, output_dim=64),
    tf.keras.layers.LSTM(64),
    tf.keras.layers.BatchNormalization(),
    tf.keras.layers.Dense(1, activation='sigmoid')
])
```

Training and Evaluation

Let us compile, train, and evaluate one of the models with regularization. You will use the model with L2 regularization for this demonstration.

```
model.compile(optimizer='adam', loss='binary_crossentropy', metrics=['accuracy'])

history = model.fit(X_train, y_train, epochs=10, validation_data=(X_val, y_val))

test_loss, test_acc = model.evaluate(X_test, y_test)
print("Test Accuracy:", test_acc)
```

By adding regularization techniques to the LSTM model, we're controlling the complexity of the model and preventing the model from fitting the noise in the training data and encourages it to generalize well on unseen data.

Each technique has different properties and effects on the model, and their performance might vary depending on the particular problem and dataset. Often, experimenting with different combinations and hyperparameters is necessary to find the most effective regularization strategy for a specific task.

In practice, regularization is a crucial step in developing robust machine learning models, especially in scenarios where the dataset might have a high degree of noise, or when the model has a large number of parameters, making it prone to overfitting. By understanding and applying these techniques, one can develop models that perform well not only on the training data but also on unseen examples, increasing the overall reliability and usability of the model.

Data Augmentation

Data augmentation is a powerful technique in the domain of deep learning, particularly beneficial when dealing with small or imbalanced datasets. By applying various transformations to the existing data, we can artificially increase the size of the training dataset, enrich its diversity, and mitigate the risk of overfitting. Although primarily used in image processing, data augmentation can also be applied to other types of data such as text and audio.

Image Data Augmentation

Image data augmentation is critical for creating diverse and robust computer vision models by synthetically expanding datasets. Augmentation artificially introduces new variations to training images that model real-world transformations. This exposes models to a wider range of realistic data during training and reduces overfitting. Modern computer vision models are powered by huge datasets that leverage diverse augmentation strategies. Here we explore common techniques:

Geometric Transformations

Applying geometric transformations is a popular technique to modify position, orientation and scale:

- Rotation: Randomly rotating images teach rotational invariance e.g. 45°, 90°, 180° etc.
- Translation: Shifting the image horizontally and vertically simulates position changes.
- Flipping: Flipping images left-right or up-down doubles the training set size while teaching mirror invariance.
- Scaling: Zooming in and out on the image helps learn scale invariance. Nearest neighbor or bilinear interpolation are used.
- Shearing: Skewing the image along the X or Y axis introduces projective distortions.
- Cropping: Extracting random crops from images focused learning on objects parts as well as full views.

Color Space Augmentation

Altering color spaces tests model sensitivity to lighting and environmental changes:

- Contrast: Increasing or decreasing contrast mimics lighting variances. Histogram equalization can improve contrast.
- Brightness: Adding or subtracting values from pixels simulates brighter or darker

conditions.

- Hue Saturation: Varying hue and saturation introduces new color representations of the same scene.
- Noise: Injecting random noise into images simulates sensor noise and graininess.

Combining Multiple Augmentations

Chaining together augmentations like random rotation, crops, hue adjustment, and horizontal flips generates exponentially more variations. Order matters - applying cropping after rotation gives different outputs than vice versa.

Contextual and Modality Augmentation

For modalities like medical imaging or lidar data, augmentations should model anatomical/contextual variations rather than generic noise:

- Domain-specific noise: Add noise correlated to scanner sensitivity vs generic noise.
- Physically valid distortions: Use elastic deformations to simulate tissue warping.
- Modality-to-modality: Cross-modality training like PET-CT or MRI-X Ray.

Implementing Image Data Augmentation in TensorFlow

Using TensorFlow, you can easily apply these augmentations. Below is an example of how to do it:

```
from tensorflow.keras.preprocessing.image import ImageDataGenerator

datagen = ImageDataGenerator(
    rotation_range=20,
    width_shift_range=0.2,
    height_shift_range=0.2,
    shear_range=0.2,
    zoom_range=0.2,
    horizontal_flip=True
)

datagen.fit(X_train)
```

Text Data Augmentation

Data augmentation is vital for expanding limited training sets, especially in modalities like text and audio that have complex underlying structure and semantics. Creative augmentation techniques are required that preserve meaning while introducing variability.

For text data, possible augmentations include:

- Paraphrasing: Rewriting sentences or paragraphs to express the same meaning using different words and grammatical constructions. This teaches models linguistic variability.
- Synonym Swapping: Strategically replacing words with their synonyms based on semantic similarity. Maintains meaning while varying lexicon.
- Grammar Variations: Altering syntax via changes in tense, active/passive voice, pronouns etc. Keeps meaning intact.
- Typos and Misspellings: Introducing plausible typos, misspellings teaches models to handle noisy real-world text. Should mimic authentic errors.
- Back Translation: Translating non-English text to other languages and back to English induces changes while preserving meaning.
- Knowledge Augmentation: Incorporating external knowledge to expand entities, concepts and relations mentioned in text.

For audio, potential augmentations include:

- Volume Modulation: Altering volume levels simulates changes in recording conditions, speaker loudness etc.
- Speed Adjustment: Modifying playback speed within intelligible limits creates new variations.
- Noise Injection: Adding ambient noise like footsteps, music, rain etc. at realistic signal-to-noise levels.
- Bandpass Filtering: Selectively filtering out high/low frequencies mimics audio recorded through different systems.
- Chaining: Concatenating audio clips together teaches segmenting relevant signals from context.

Crucially, augmentations must model variability authentic to the end use cases. Generic noise doesn't help if real distortions are systematic. Augmentation strategies should thus match real-world factors affecting each modality. Used judiciously, data augmentation unlocks substantial gains in model robustness, generalization and accuracy for text, audio and other modalities.

Overall, data augmentation is an indispensable tool in modern machine learning. By creatively leveraging augmentation techniques, practitioners can not only enhance model robustness but also explore model behavior under various conditions, leading to insights into model strengths and weaknesses. It's a dynamic field with ongoing research, and new methods and approaches continue to emerge.

Dropout and Batch Normalization

Dropout

Dropout is a regularization technique where randomly selected neurons are ignored or "dropped out" during training, reducing the model's reliance on any specific neuron. Dropout works by randomly setting a fraction of the input units to 0 during training, helping prevent overfitting. The dropout rate is the fraction of the input units to drop.

Implementing Dropout

Below is how to apply Dropout in a neural network using TensorFlow:

```
from tensorflow.keras.models import Sequential
from tensorflow.keras.layers import Dense, Dropout

model = Sequential([
    Dense(64, activation='relu', input_shape=(input_shape,)),
    Dropout(0.5),  # Dropout layer with 50% dropout rate
    Dense(10, activation='softmax')
])
```

The Dropout layer takes the dropout rate as an argument, e.g., 0.5 means 50% of the neurons will be dropped out during training.

Using Dropout with CNN

For Convolutional Neural Networks, the same layer can be added between convolutional and dense layers:

```
from tensorflow.keras.layers import Conv2D

model = Sequential([
    Conv2D(32, (3, 3), activation='relu', input_shape=(28, 28, 1)),
    Dropout(0.25),  # 25% dropout rate
    # Further layers...
])
```

Batch Normalization

Batch Normalization normalizes the output of a previous activation layer by subtracting the batch mean and dividing by the batch standard deviation. Batch Normalization addresses the problem of internal covariate shift, where the distribution of inputs changes during training. By normalizing the inputs to each layer, it can improve training speed and stability.

Implementing Batch Normalization

Below is how to apply Batch Normalization in a neural network:

```
from tensorflow.keras.layers import BatchNormalization

model = Sequential([
    Dense(64, activation='relu', input_shape=(input_shape,)),
    BatchNormalization(),
    Dense(10, activation='softmax')
])
```

The BatchNormalization layer can be added after a dense or convolutional layer, before the activation function.

Using Batch Normalization with CNN

In CNNs, Batch Normalization can be applied in a similar fashion:

```
model = Sequential([
    Conv2D(32, (3, 3), input_shape=(28, 28, 1)),
    BatchNormalization(),
    Activation('relu'),
    # Further layers...
])
```

Combining Dropout and Batch Normalization

These techniques can be combined within the same model to achieve even better performance. Following is an example:

```
model = Sequential([
    Dense(64, activation='relu', input_shape=(input_shape,)),
    Dropout(0.5),
    BatchNormalization(),
    Dense(10, activation='softmax')
])
```

By integrating these techniques into the model, the model becomes more robust and generalizes well to unseen data. Practical examples provided above can be easily applied to previous models and datasets for improved performance.

Early Stopping

Overview

Overfitting happens when a model performs well on the training data but poorly on unseen or validation data. As the epochs increase, the model continues to minimize the loss function for the training data but may start to perform worse on the validation data. Early stopping is another regularization technique that helps prevent overfitting in machine learning models. Unlike Dropout and Batch Normalization, which alter the architecture or training process itself, early stopping focuses on halting the training process at the right time.

Early stopping addresses this by monitoring a specified metric (e.g., validation loss) and stops the training process once that metric has stopped improving.

How Does Early Stopping Work?

Early stopping requires a division of data into training, validation, and test sets. During training, the model's performance is evaluated on the validation set. If the performance stops improving (or even degrades) for a specified number of epochs, the training is halted.

You can implement early stopping in TensorFlow using the EarlyStopping callback. Below is how to do it:

- Import EarlyStopping: You'll need to import the EarlyStopping class from Keras callbacks.

- Create an EarlyStopping Instance: You need to decide on the metric to monitor (e.g., val_loss), how much change to consider an improvement (min_delta), and how many epochs with no improvement before stopping (patience).

- Add the Callback to Model Training: When you call the fit method on your model, include the early stopping instance in the callbacks parameter.

Sample Program: Implementing Early Stopping using Neural Network

Following is a practical example using a neural network:

```
from tensorflow.keras.callbacks import EarlyStopping

# Define the early stopping criteria
early_stopping = EarlyStopping(monitor='val_loss', patience=5, min_delta=0.01)

# Compile and fit the model
model.compile(optimizer='adam', loss='sparse_categorical_crossentropy',
metrics=['accuracy'])
model.fit(X_train, y_train, epochs=100, validation_data=(X_val, y_val),
callbacks=[early_stopping])
```

In the above sample program:

- monitor='val_loss' specifies that we're monitoring the validation loss.
- patience=5 means that training will continue for five more epochs after no improvement is seen.
- min_delta=0.01 indicates that an absolute change of less than 0.01 in the monitored metric is considered no improvement.

Early stopping is commonly used in conjunction with other regularization techniques, like Dropout and Batch Normalization, to prevent overfitting. By halting training at the right time, it saves computational resources and often results in a model that generalizes better to unseen data.

The early stopping technique is versatile and can be applied to various types of neural networks, including Convolutional Neural Networks (CNNs), Recurrent Neural Networks (RNNs), and LSTMs. The approach remains the same, with adjustments made according to the specific architecture and problem being solved. Whether working on image recognition or sequence prediction, incorporating early stopping helps in achieving a balance between underfitting and overfitting.

Cross Validation

Overview

Cross-validation is a resampling procedure used to evaluate machine learning models on a limited data sample. It ensures that every observation from the original dataset has the chance of appearing in the training and test set. This makes cross-validation particularly useful when the available data is limited. Among the most popular cross-validation techniques is k-fold cross-validation.

In k-fold cross-validation, the original sample is randomly partitioned into k equal-sized subsamples. Of the k subsamples, a single subsample is retained as the validation data, and the remaining k-1 subsamples are used as training data. This process is repeated k times, with each of the k subsamples used exactly once as the validation data.

Implementing K-fold Cross-Validation

- Divide the Dataset: Divide the dataset into k equal parts or "folds." If the dataset contains 1000 examples and k=10, then each fold would contain 100 examples.
- Train and Validate: For each unique group:
- Take the group as a validation set.
- Take the remaining groups as a training set.
- Fit a model on the training set and evaluate it on the validation set.
- Retain the evaluation score and discard the model.

Sample Program: Applying K-fold Cross-Validation

Let us take a previously discussed example of classifying text and apply k-fold cross-validation using TensorFlow and scikit-learn.

Import Libraries

```
from sklearn.model_selection import KFold
from tensorflow.keras.models import Sequential
from tensorflow.keras.layers import Embedding, LSTM, Dense
```

Define the Model

Create a function to define the model, as it will be created multiple times for each fold.

```
def create_model():
    model = Sequential()
    model.add(Embedding(input_dim=vocab_size, output_dim=128))
    model.add(LSTM(64))
    model.add(Dense(1, activation='sigmoid'))
    model.compile(optimizer='adam', loss='binary_crossentropy', metrics=['accuracy'])
    return model
```

Apply K-fold Cross-Validation

```
kf = KFold(n_splits=10, shuffle=True)
scores = []

for train_index, val_index in kf.split(X):
    X_train, X_val = X[train_index], X[val_index]
    y_train, y_val = y[train_index], y[val_index]

    model – create_model()
    model.fit(X_train, y_train, epochs=5)

    loss, accuracy = model.evaluate(X_val, y_val)
    scores.append(accuracy)

print(f'Mean Accuracy: {np.mean(scores)}')
```

Here, the data is split into 10 folds, and for each fold, the model is trained and validated. The mean accuracy is then printed at the end.

K-fold cross-validation is an essential tool in the model evaluation process, providing a more reliable assessment of a model's performance. Integrating k-fold cross-validation in your workflows provides you with a better understanding of how your models are likely to perform on unseen data, leading to more confident decision-making in model selection and tuning.

Summary

In this chapter, we delved into the key concepts of overfitting and underfitting, understanding the importance of striking a balance between model complexity and performance on unseen data. We explored regularization techniques that can mitigate overfitting, including L1 and L2 regularization, exploring them with practical examples. The concept of data augmentation was discussed as a means to artificially expand the dataset, providing the model with "new" training examples.

Further, we covered dropout and batch normalization. While dropout prevents overfitting by randomly setting a fraction of the input units to zero at each update during training time, batch normalization normalizes the activations of a given input volume before passing it through the activation function. Early stopping was introduced as a way to cease training once the model's performance stops improving on a held-out validation dataset, thereby preventing overfitting.

We also learned about cross-validation, a robust technique for assessing a model's performance when the data sample is limited. We explored how to apply it practically, dividing the dataset into 'k' subsets and training the model k times on different combinations of these subsets. This chapter provided practical insights and techniques to prevent overfitting, enhance model generalization, and ensure that models perform well on unseen data. These concepts and practices form the foundation of building robust and reliable machine learning models and are essential in the toolkit of anyone working in the field.

CHAPTER 8: ADVANCED NEURAL NETWORKS FOR NLP

Advanced Neural Networks Overview

Traditional LSTM processes data from the beginning to the end. Bidirectional LSTM (BiLSTM) takes the concept further by processing the data in both directions. By having two LSTMs, one processing the data from left to right and the other from right to left, BiLSTM can capture information from the past and the future around a specific part of the data. It is especially useful in NLP tasks like sentiment analysis or translation where context from both sides of a word or sequence is beneficial.

In sequence-to-sequence tasks like translation, the attention mechanism helps the model to focus on certain parts of the input when producing the output, similar to how humans pay attention to specific portions of input when reading or listening. This "attention" enables the model to remember relevant parts of the input sequence when decoding, making the model more effective in handling long sequences. Then, the transformer model is a novel take on sequence modeling that leverages attention mechanisms entirely, without relying on recurrence. Unlike RNNs, which process sequences step by step, transformers process all the elements in the sequence simultaneously. This parallelization allows for more efficient training and has led to significant improvements in tasks like translation and text summarization.

We will also discuss GANs that consist of two networks, a generator and a discriminator, that are trained together. The generator tries to create data that is similar to some genuine data, while the discriminator tries to distinguish between real and fake data. When applied to text, GANs can generate new text that follows the pattern and complexity of a given dataset. This is a challenging application, as text data is discrete, and small changes can have a significant impact on meaning. Apart from the above, there is something called as Capsule Networks (or CapsNets), an exciting development in neural network architecture. Traditional CNNs might lose important hierarchical spatial relationships between simple and complex objects in an image. Capsule networks preserve these relationships and are designed to recognize objects in images via their parts and the relationships between them.

Together, these advanced aspects of neural networks represent the cutting edge of deep learning research and application. They offer innovative ways to process, understand, and generate sequential and spatial data, and their practical applications are numerous and growing. In subsequent sections, you will explore each of these topics in detail, providing the necessary foundation and insights to understand and utilize these powerful techniques.

Understanding Bidirectional LSTM

Bidirectional Long Short-Term Memory (BiLSTM) networks are a variant of traditional LSTM networks, a special kind of Recurrent Neural Networks (RNNs). They have shown significant advantages over standard LSTMs, particularly in tasks where context from both earlier and later parts of the input sequence contributes to the understanding of that sequence.

Importance

Improved Context Understanding

In many sequence processing tasks like text or speech analysis, understanding the full context is crucial. Standard LSTMs process sequences in one direction, either from beginning to end or vice versa. BiLSTMs, however, process the sequence in both directions simultaneously, capturing information from both the past and the future relative to each point in the sequence. This two-way analysis enhances the understanding of context, which is particularly beneficial for tasks like sentiment analysis or entity recognition.

Robust Performance in Various Tasks

The symmetric structure of BiLSTMs allows them to outperform standard LSTMs in various tasks, such as speech recognition, part-of-speech tagging, and protein structure prediction. This is largely due to their ability to leverage information from the entire sequence when making predictions about any particular part of it.

Architecture

Two LSTM Layers

A BiLSTM consists of two LSTM layers processing the input sequence in opposite directions. One LSTM processes the sequence from the beginning to the end (forward pass), and the other processes it from the end to the beginning (backward pass).

Concatenating or Combining Outputs

The outputs of the forward and backward passes can be concatenated or combined in various ways, such as summing, averaging, or using more complex operations. This process forms a new sequence that captures information from both directions.

Sequence Processing

Like standard LSTMs, BiLSTMs can process sequences of arbitrary lengths. The forward and backward LSTMs share parameters, ensuring symmetry in how they process the sequence.

Hidden States and Cell States

Similar to standard LSTMs, each BiLSTM unit has a hidden state and a cell state. The hidden state captures short-term dependencies, while the cell state captures long-term dependencies. The bidirectional structure ensures that these states capture dependencies from both directions.

Connection with Other Layers

The combined outputs of the forward and backward LSTMs can be used as inputs to other layers, such as fully connected layers or other RNN layers. This makes BiLSTMs highly flexible and integrable into complex deep learning architectures.

BiLSTMs have become standard in many sequence processing tasks. In Natural Language Processing (NLP), they are used in translation, summarization, and question answering. In speech processing, they are applied to speech-to-text conversion and speaker recognition. Their ability to capture complex dependencies in sequences makes them a valuable tool for researchers and practitioners working with time-series data. Their symmetric architecture and flexibility in combining the forward and backward passes make them an adaptable and effective tool for many sequence-based tasks. Their success in various fields demonstrates the importance and effectiveness of considering the full context of a sequence in both directions.

Sample Program: BiLSTM for Sentiment Analysis

Building on our previous example of sentiment analysis, let us practically implement a Bidirectional LSTM (BiLSTM) model for this task. You will use TensorFlow, and the code will follow the process of preparing the data, defining the BiLSTM model, training it, and finally using it to predict sentiment.

Data Preparation

Since we are continuing from a previously discussed sentiment analysis application, you will assume that you already have your text data preprocessed and divided into training and validation sets. You will use tokenization and padding to prepare the data for the BiLSTM model:

```
from tensorflow.keras.preprocessing.text import Tokenizer
from tensorflow.keras.preprocessing.sequence import pad_sequences

# Tokenization
tokenizer = Tokenizer(num_words=vocab_size, oov_token="<OOV>")
tokenizer.fit_on_texts(training_sentences)
word_index = tokenizer.word_index

# Convert to sequences
train_sequences = tokenizer.texts_to_sequences(training_sentences)
val_sequences = tokenizer.texts_to_sequences(validation_sentences)

# Padding
train_padded = pad_sequences(train_sequences, maxlen=max_length, padding="post",
```

```
truncating="post")
val_padded = pad_sequences(val_sequences, maxlen=max_length, padding="post",
truncating="post")
```

Model Definition

Let us define a BiLSTM model. This model will have an Embedding layer followed by a Bidirectional LSTM layer, and then a Dense layer for output:

```
from tensorflow.keras.models import Sequential
from tensorflow.keras.layers import Embedding, Bidirectional, LSTM, Dense

model = Sequential([
    Embedding(vocab_size, embedding_dim, input_length=max_length),
    Bidirectional(LSTM(64, return_sequences=True)),
    Bidirectional(LSTM(32)),
    Dense(24, activation='relu'),
    Dense(1, activation='sigmoid')
])

model.compile(loss='binary_crossentropy', optimizer='adam', metrics=['accuracy'])
```

Training the Model

You will train the model on our prepared training data:

```
history = model.fit(
    train_padded,
    training_labels,
    epochs=10,
    validation_data=(val_padded, validation_labels)
)
```

Model Evaluation and Prediction

You can evaluate the model on your test set:

```
loss, accuracy = model.evaluate(test_padded, test_labels)
print("Test accuracy:", accuracy)
```

For predicting sentiment, you can use:

```
text = ["Your input text here"]
sequence = tokenizer.texts_to_sequences(text)
padded = pad_sequences(sequence, maxlen=max_length, padding="post",
truncating="post")
prediction = model.predict(padded)
```

The above code will return a value between 0 and 1, representing the predicted sentiment for the input text.

BiLSTMs enable the model to understand the context from both previous and future tokens in the text. By using a BiLSTM in our sentiment analysis task, the model has the capacity to identify nuanced relationships in the text and potentially achieve higher accuracy. This dual directional understanding makes BiLSTMs suitable for tasks where the complete context is essential for accurate predictions, such as in our sentiment analysis application.

Attention Mechanism for seq2seq Models

The attention mechanism is a pivotal advancement in the field of neural networks, specifically in seq2seq tasks such as machine translation, text summarization, and speech recognition. It is designed to help the model focus on relevant parts of the input when producing the output, similar to how human attention works when we focus on specific aspects of our surroundings.

Basic Fundamentals

Traditional seq2seq models without attention suffer from a limitation known as the fixed-size bottleneck. The encoder compresses the entire input sequence into a fixed-size vector called the context vector, and the decoder uses this vector to generate the output sequence. This approach is problematic for longer sequences, as compressing all information into a fixed-size vector leads to loss of information.

The attention mechanism overcomes this limitation by allowing the decoder to refer back to the entire input sequence, rather than just the fixed-size context vector. This is achieved by dynamically focusing on different parts of the input sequence as the output sequence is generated.

How Attention Works?

Alignment Scores

For each time step in the decoder, the model computes a score representing the relationship between the input at that step and every other step in the source sequence. Commonly used scoring functions include dot product, scaled dot product, and concatenation followed by a feed-forward network.

Softmax Layer

These scores are passed through a softmax layer, converting them into probabilities. These probabilities determine the weight given to each corresponding encoder hidden state. Essentially, higher scores lead to more attention being paid to specific parts of the input.

Context Vector

The model calculates a weighted sum of the encoder hidden states, using the softmax probabilities as weights. This creates a context vector for each time step in the decoder, dynamically representing relevant parts of the input.

Output Generation

The context vector is concatenated or merged with the hidden state of the decoder, providing additional context when generating the output token for that time step.

Types of Attention

Global Attention

This type involves attention over all the encoder's hidden states. It can be computationally expensive for very long sequences.

Local Attention

Here, attention is paid only to a subset of the encoder's hidden states, based on the current state of the decoder. It's more computationally efficient.

Impact on Seq2Seq Models

The attention mechanism has brought a significant positive impact on the performance of seq2seq models. Some key benefits include:

- Improved Handling of Long Sequences: By allowing the model to focus on relevant parts of the input dynamically, it reduces the information loss that occurs when compressing long sequences into a fixed-size vector.
- Interpretability: Attention weights can be visualized, offering insights into what parts of the input the model is focusing on at each step.

- Enhanced Modeling of Dependencies: The mechanism enables the model to capture complex relationships within the input data, even over longer distances within the sequence.

By mimicking the way human attention operates, attention mechanism has enabled models to handle complex sequences more accurately and transparently, leading to significant advancements in various NLP tasks. The adaptability of attention mechanisms has spurred innovation and exploration into various attention-based architectures, transforming the landscape of sequence modeling in deep learning.

Sample Program: Attention Mechanism for Language Translation

The attention mechanism greatly improves the performance of sequence-to-sequence models, particularly in tasks like language translation. In this sample program, you will practically implement an attention mechanism using TensorFlow for a language translation task. You will make use of the transformer architecture, which employs attention heavily. Let us continue with the previously used language translation task and extend it with attention.

Setting up Environment & Data Prep

First, import the necessary libraries and dependencies:

```
import tensorflow as tf
from tensorflow.keras.layers import Layer, Embedding, Dense
from tensorflow.keras.models import Model
import numpy as np
```

Load the dataset that you've previously used for language translation. You can preprocess the data in the same way, including tokenization and padding.

Attention Mechanism Implementation

The attention mechanism will be implemented as a custom layer in TensorFlow. Below is how you can define a scaled dot-product attention function:

```
def scaled_dot_product_attention(query, key, value, mask=None):
    matmul_qk = tf.matmul(query, key, transpose_b=True)
    d_k = tf.cast(tf.shape(key)[-1], tf.float32)
```

```
    scaled_attention_logits = matmul_qk / tf.math.sqrt(d_k)
    if mask is not None:
        scaled_attention_logits += (mask * -1e9)
    attention_weights = tf.nn.softmax(scaled_attention_logits, axis=-1)
    output = tf.matmul(attention_weights, value)
    return output, attention_weights
```

To allow the model to jointly attend to information at different positions, we implement multi-head attention as a layer:

```
class MultiHeadAttention(Layer):
    def __init__(self, d_model, num_heads):
        super(MultiHeadAttention, self).__init__()
        self.num_heads = num_heads
        self.d_model = d_model
        self.depth = d_model // self.num_heads

        self.wq = Dense(d_model)
        self.wk = Dense(d_model)
        self.wv = Dense(d_model)
        self.dense = Dense(d_model)

    def split_heads(self, x, batch_size):
        x = tf.reshape(x, (batch_size, -1, self.num_heads, self.depth))
        return tf.transpose(x, perm=[0, 2, 1, 3])

    def call(self, v, k, q, mask):
        batch_size = tf.shape(q)[0]
        q = self.split_heads(self.wq(q), batch_size)
        k = self.split_heads(self.wk(k), batch_size)
        v = self.split_heads(self.wv(v), batch_size)
        output, attention_weights = scaled_dot_product_attention(q, k, v, mask)
        output = tf.transpose(output, perm=[0, 2, 1, 3])
        output = tf.reshape(output, (batch_size, -1, self.d_model))
```

```
    output = self.dense(output)
    return output, attention_weights
```

Compile and train the transformer model using the previously preprocessed data for language translation. And then, use the trained transformer model to translate new sentences. You can also visualize the attention weights to understand what parts of the input the model is focusing on while translating.

Transformer Architecture

The transformer architecture has fundamentally changed the field of natural language processing and many other applications that work with sequences. Introduced by Vaswani et al. in the paper "Attention is All You Need" in 2017, the transformer does away with recurrence entirely and instead relies solely on attention mechanisms to draw global dependencies between input and output.

Overview

The transformer consists of two main parts: the encoder and the decoder. Both are composed of multiple layers (commonly 6) of identical architecture but with different learned parameters. The following describes the primary components of this architecture:

Encoder

- Input Embedding: Each input token is represented by a vector obtained through word embedding.
- Positional Encoding: Since the transformer doesn't have any recurrent elements, positional encodings are added to give the model information about the position of the words in the sequence.
- Multi-Head Attention Layer: This allows the model to focus on different parts of the input sequence when encoding a particular part of it.
- Feed-Forward Neural Network: A fully connected feed-forward network is used within the encoder, followed by layer normalization.

Each of these above elements are repeated N times, where N is the number of layers in the encoder.

Decoder

The decoder has a similar structure to the encoder but with an additional multi-head attention layer that attends to the output of the encoder.

- Output Embedding: This transforms the output sequence to vectors.

- Positional Encoding: Similar to the encoder, the positional encoding is added.
- Multi-Head Attention Layer: Attends to the decoder's input (the target sequence).
- Multi-Head Attention Layer: This second attention layer attends to the encoder's output.
- Feed-Forward Neural Network: Similar to the encoder, there's a feed-forward network and layer normalization.

Multi-Head Attention Mechanism

The multi-head attention mechanism is at the core of the transformer architecture. Below is how it functions:

- Splitting Heads: The input is divided into multiple heads, which allows the network to simultaneously attend to different parts of the input.
- Scaled Dot-Product Attention: For each head, the attention scores are computed by taking the dot product of the query and key, followed by scaling and applying a softmax function.
- Combining Heads: The results from each head are concatenated and passed through a linear layer.

The use of multiple heads enhances the expressive ability of the attention mechanism, enabling it to capture various aspects of the relationship between different parts of the input sequence.

Position-wise Feed-Forward Networks

Each layer of the encoder and decoder also contains a feed forward neural network that is applied to each position separately and identically. These networks consist of two linear transformations with a ReLU activation in between. Positional encodings are added to the input embeddings at the bottom of the encoder and decoder stacks. These encodings provide information about the positions of the tokens in the sequence. The authors of the transformer paper used sinusoidal functions for these encodings, but learned positional encodings are also common. The transformer model is trained end-to-end using a standard supervised learning approach. The objective is typically to minimize the negative log-likelihood of the target sequence given the input sequence. In the case of language modeling or translation, this is often achieved using cross-entropy loss.

Models like BERT, GPT-2, and GPT-3 have built upon the original transformer architecture, demonstrating its adaptability and effectiveness in handling complex sequential data. By focusing on the relationships between all parts of the input, rather than processing it one step at a time, the transformer achieves impressive performance in many tasks. Its design has inspired a wave of research and innovation, further extending its impact across various domains of machine learning and artificial intelligence.

Sample Program: Implementing Named Entity Recognition using Transformer

Named Entity Recognition (NER) is a subtask of Information Extraction that classifies named entities into predefined categories such as the names of persons, organizations, locations, expressions of times, quantities, and more. In this illustration, you will walk through the process of implementing NER using the transformer architecture with a step-by-step explanation.

Importing Necessary Libraries

You will be using the Hugging Face Transformers library, which makes it easy to work with transformer models. First, import the required libraries.

```
from transformers import BertTokenizer, BertForTokenClassification
import torch
```

Here, we are importing the BERT tokenizer and model specifically designed for token classification.

Loading Pre-trained Model

You will use a pre-trained BERT model that is fine-tuned for the NER task. You can load the tokenizer and model as follows:

```
tokenizer = BertTokenizer.from_pretrained('dbmdz/bert-large-cased-finetuned-conll03-
english')
model = BertForTokenClassification.from_pretrained('dbmdz/bert-large-cased-
finetuned-conll03-english')
```

We load a pre-trained BERT model that has been fine-tuned on a standard NER dataset (CoNLL-03). This model understands English language entities.

Preprocessing the Input

Tokenize your input sentence and prepare it as a PyTorch tensor.

```
input_sentence = "Steve Jobs founded Apple Inc. in Cupertino."
inputs = tokenizer(input_sentence, return_tensors="pt", padding=True,
```

```
truncation=True)
```

The tokenizer converts the raw text into a format that is compatible with the model. This includes converting words into their corresponding IDs, adding special tokens, and handling padding and truncation.

Forward Pass

Perform a forward pass through the model to get the predictions. This returns the hidden states of the model, from which you can derive the predicted token classifications.

```
outputs = model(**inputs)
predictions = torch.argmax(outputs.logits, dim=2)
```

The forward pass generates predictions for each token in the input sentence. The logits represent the raw prediction scores for each possible category (e.g., person, organization, etc.) for each token.

Decoding the Predictions

Use the tokenizer to convert the predictions into a human-readable format.

```
for word, prediction in zip(input_sentence.split(), predictions[0].numpy()):
    print(f"{word}: {model.config.id2label[prediction]}")
```

Here, we interpret the predictions by converting the predicted IDs back into their corresponding named entity labels.

This method is quite effective in applications like content categorization, automating CRM notes, customer support ticket tagging, and more. NER can also play a crucial role in enhancing search algorithms, summarization, and also in building efficient question-answering systems. This practical demonstration highlights the ease and efficiency of using transformer architecture, specifically a pre-trained BERT model, for Named Entity Recognition.

Generative Adversarial Networks

Generative Adversarial Networks (GANs) have transformed the landscape of generative modeling and deep learning since their introduction in 2014. Through an innovative adversarial framework of two competing neural networks, GANs have demonstrated immense potential to generate remarkably realistic synthetic data that captures the nuances and complexities of real-world data distributions. In this exploration, you will dive into the fundamental concepts, architecture, training techniques, applications, challenges, and innovations around GANs.

At its core, a GAN consists of two neural networks - a Generator (G) and a Discriminator (D) - engaged in a minimax adversarial game. The Generator attempts to create synthetic data that is indistinguishable from real data, while the Discriminator aims to identify which data instances are real and which are fake. This rivalry pushes both networks to improve until the Generator can reliably produce high fidelity artificial data. Now let us unpack the key components that enable this process.

Architecture

The architecture of a GAN is deceptively simple, consisting solely of the Generator and Discriminator networks. However, the capabilities emerge from how they interact during the adversarial training process.

- Generator (G): The Generator is typically a deconvolutional neural network that maps samples from a simple latent distribution such as a Gaussian into synthetic data samples. It starts with a random noise vector z as input, then applies a series of upsampling and convolutional layers to increase spatial dimensions and construct more complex representations until it outputs the desired synthetic data like an image. The goal is to estimate the true data distribution and generate samples that reside on the authentic data manifold.

- Discriminator (D): The Discriminator is usually a convolutional neural network that classifies its inputs as real or fake - essentially a binary classifier. It takes either real data samples from the training dataset or fake samples from the Generator as input. By applying a series of convolutional and downsampling layers, it outputs a probability score between 0 and 1 indicating how likely the input is real. It aims to distinguish real data from the Generator's synthetic outputs.

The architectures can vary, but the GAN paradigm remains the same - G trying to fool D and D trying to catch G's fakes. Now let us explore how adversarial training allows them to achieve this.

Training Process

GAN training is a delicate balancing act requiring careful coordination of the Generator and Discriminators objectives.

Following are the key steps:

1. Initialize G and D with random weights. They start with no knowledge of the data distribution.

2. Train D on real samples from the dataset, adjusting parameters so it can recognize real data.
3. Generate fake samples with the current G and train D to identify them as fake.
4. Train G to make its outputs more realistic to fool D better on the next iteration.
5. Repeat steps 2-4, altering real and fake training in tandem until convergence criteria are met.

This iterative adversarial training loop allows G and D to evolve together until the Generator can reliably produce realistic artificial data. The loss functions for each player also require careful specification.

Loss Functions

The loss functions for G and D are designed to reflect their competing objectives:

- Discriminator Loss: D wants to maximize the probability of correctly classifying reals and fakes. This can be represented as the binary cross-entropy loss:

$$LD = -E[\log D(x)] - E[\log(1 - D(G(z)))]$$

where x is from the real dataset and z is Gaussian noise input to G.

- Generator Loss: G wants to minimize D's ability to identify its outputs as fake. This can be expressed as:

$$LG = -E[\log D(G(z))]$$

In other words, G aims to maximize the error rate of D.

Balancing these opposing loss functions is critical for healthy competition and convergence. Various techniques like gradient penalties or alternative loss formulations have also been proposed to improve training. But the basic idea remains the same - an adversarial tug-of-war.

GANs have unlocked revolutionary capabilities across diverse domains thanks to their ability to discover data distributions. The given below are some of the most prominent applications:

- Image generation: Creating photorealistic images, artworks, editing images by modifying attributes.
- Data augmentation: Generating synthetic training data similar to real samples to overcome scarce datasets.
- Text-to-image synthesis: Generating images from textual descriptions using conditioned GANs.

- Drug discovery: Designing new molecular structures with desired pharmacological properties.
- Super-resolution: Enhancing image resolution far beyond native scales using SRGANs and other variants.
- Anomaly detection: Detecting abnormal data points that differ from expected distributions.
- Time series generation: Producing realistic time series such as stock market data based on historical patterns.

These above highlight the remarkable versatility of GANs for realizing generative goals. But it doesn't come without unique challenges.

To sum up, Generative Adversarial Networks fundamentally expanded the possibilities for generative deep learning. Through the adversarial interaction between a Generator that creates artificial data and a Discriminator that evaluates realism, GANs can discover and mimic the fine details of real-world data distributions with remarkable fidelity. Architectural innovations paired with improved training techniques have also unlocked myriad applications from creating artistic masterpieces to designing new drugs. Despite ongoing challenges in stable training, GANs remain one of the most exciting frontiers of machine learning research with enormous future potential. The possibilities are limited only by human imagination and innovation.

Sample Program: Applying GANs on Text

Applying Generative Adversarial Networks (GANs) to text data presents some unique challenges, primarily because text data is discrete and thus gradients cannot be easily back-propagated through the text-generation process. However, there are techniques and architectures designed to overcome these challenges. Below, you will go through a practical example using a simple text dataset and work with a conditional GAN structure to generate text.

Define the Problem

Suppose we want to generate new sentences similar to those in a given text corpus, such as generating new poetry lines based on a collection of poems.

Preprocessing the Data

You will use a one-hot encoding technique to represent our text. This means that each word will be represented as a binary vector where the position of the word in our vocabulary is marked as 1, and the rest of the vector is filled with 0s.

```
from keras.preprocessing.text import Tokenizer
from keras.preprocessing.sequence import pad_sequences
```

```
# Tokenize the text
tokenizer = Tokenizer()
tokenizer.fit_on_texts(corpus)
vocab_size = len(tokenizer.word_index) + 1

# Convert text to sequences
sequences = tokenizer.texts_to_sequences(corpus)
sequences = pad_sequences(sequences, maxlen=max_length, padding='post')

# Convert sequences to one-hot encoding
def to_one_hot(sequences, vocab_size):
    one_hot = np.zeros((len(sequences), max_length, vocab_size))
    for i, sequence in enumerate(sequences):
        for j, word in enumerate(sequence):
            one_hot[i, j, word] = 1
    return one_hot

X = to_one_hot(sequences, vocab_size)
```

Build the GAN

The Generator takes a random noise vector and a condition (e.g., a category or a prompt) as input and generates a sequence of one-hot encoded words.

```
from keras.models import Model
from keras.layers import Input, Dense, Reshape, Concatenate

def build_generator(vocab_size, max_length):
    noise = Input(shape=(noise_dim,))
    condition = Input(shape=(condition_dim,))
    merged_input = Concatenate()([noise, condition])

    x = Dense(256, activation='relu')(merged_input)
```

```
    x = Dense(vocab_size * max_length, activation='softmax')(x)
    x = Reshape((max_length, vocab_size))(x)

    model = Model([noise, condition], x)
    return model
```

The Discriminator takes a sequence of one-hot encoded words and a condition as input and determines whether the sequence is real or generated.

```
from keras.layers import Flatten

def build_discriminator(vocab_size, max_length):
    text = Input(shape=(max_length, vocab_size))
    condition = Input(shape=(condition_dim,))
    flat_text = Flatten()(text)
    merged_input = Concatenate()([flat_text, condition])

    x = Dense(256, activation='relu')(merged_input)
    x = Dense(1, activation='sigmoid')(x)

    model = Model([text, condition], x)
    return model
```

Training the GAN

Training a GAN for text involves careful balancing of the Generator and Discriminator training. We need to alternate between training the Discriminator and the Generator.

```
# Compile the Discriminator
discriminator.compile(optimizer='adam', loss='binary_crossentropy')

# Compile the combined model
discriminator.trainable = False
combined_input = [noise, condition]
combined_output = discriminator([generator(combined_input), condition])
```

```
combined = Model(combined_input, combined_output)
combined.compile(optimizer='adam', loss='binary_crossentropy')

# Training loop
for epoch in range(epochs):
    # Train Discriminator
    ...
    # Train Generator
    ...
```

Generating Text

Once the GAN is trained, we can use the Generator to produce new text given a noise vector and a condition.

Constructing a GAN for the purpose of text generation is a challenging but ultimately rewarding process. You can create a model that generates creative and compelling text by first understanding the challenges, and then applying thoughtful solutions to address those challenges. GANs offer a potent instrument for the generation of text, making them useful not only for artistic endeavors but also for data augmentation and other applications.

Capsule Networks

Capsule Networks, also known as "CapsNets," represent a groundbreaking development in the field of deep learning, aiming to overcome some limitations of traditional Convolutional Neural Networks (CNNs). Geoffrey Hinton first introduced the concept, proposing a method to enable neural networks to understand the hierarchical spatial relationships within an image or other structured data. The following sections will describe the underlying components, working principles, and functionality of Capsule Networks.

Motivation Behind Capsule Networks

Traditional CNNs excel in detecting patterns and features in data but often lack the ability to understand spatial hierarchies and the relationships between those features. This limitation can lead to misinterpretations, especially when an object is viewed from different perspectives or orientations. Capsule Networks aim to solve this problem by encoding not only the presence of features but also their spatial orientation and relationship to one another.

Basic Components of Capsule Networks

Capsules

A capsule is a small group of neurons representing different properties of a specific feature or object, such as its position, orientation, size, and texture. Unlike traditional neurons, which only output a single scalar value, capsules output a vector. The magnitude of the vector represents the presence of a particular feature, while the orientation encodes specific properties of that feature.

Dynamic Routing

Dynamic routing is a mechanism for determining how capsules in one layer should be connected to capsules in the next layer. Unlike traditional neural networks, where connections are fixed, dynamic routing allows capsules to decide where to send their outputs based on the data. This flexible routing allows the network to recognize spatial hierarchies and relationships between features more effectively.

Architecture of Capsule Networks

Encoder (Encoding Phase)

The encoder part consists of multiple layers of capsules, often beginning with traditional convolutional layers to detect initial features. The detected features are then fed into primary capsules, followed by subsequent capsule layers.

- Convolutional Layer: Extracts basic features like edges, corners, etc.
- Primary Capsule Layer: Transforms scalar outputs into vector outputs, initiating the capsule structure.
- Digit Capsule Layer: Utilizes dynamic routing to create higher-level representations of the data.

Decoder (Reconstruction Phase)

Capsule Networks often include a decoder that reconstructs the input from the encoded representations. This reconstruction serves as a regularization method and assists in training by minimizing the difference between the input and the reconstructed output.

Dynamic Routing Algorithm

The dynamic routing algorithm is the key innovation that sets Capsule Networks apart from conventional convolutional neural networks. It establishes relationships between capsules in adjacent layers through an iterative routing process. Each capsule attempts to predict the output of capsules in the layer above using linear transformations and prediction vectors. The central idea is that if a higher level capsule is confident about the existence of a particular feature, it will assign higher coupling coefficients to the most relevant lower-level capsules during routing.

The routing algorithm involves the following key steps:

1. Initial coupling coefficients between all capsule pairs are set to zero. These coefficients determine the connection strengths.
2. Each lower-level capsule sends its output vector vo to make predictions for higher level capsules.
3. Prediction vectors are calculated between each capsule pair using weight matrices.
4. Coupling coefficients are updated between the capsule and all prediction vectors based on the agreement between them.
5. Weighted sums are computed for each higher level capsule using the coefficients and prediction vectors.
6. A non-linear squash function is applied to obtain the vector output of each higher-level capsule.
7. Steps 2-6 are repeated iteratively until the coupling coefficients stabilize.

In this way, capsules in adjacent layers build consensus on the presence of entities and learn meaningful representations of spatial relationships through dynamic routing. The number of routing iterations is a key hyperparameter. This algorithm allows Capsule Networks to selectively amplify capsules that agree while suppressing irrelevant ones. By modeling part-whole relationships, robust representations are learned that are equivariant to transformations. The dynamic routing mechanism is central to the capabilities of Capsule Networks in encoding spatial hierarchies within images or data.

Capsule Networks represent a promising advancement, offering a more nuanced understanding of spatial hierarchies and relationships within data. By encapsulating rich information in vectors and employing dynamic routing, they provide a powerful mechanism for pattern recognition and feature understanding. Though there are challenges and limitations, the ongoing research and applications of Capsule Networks hold substantial potential across various domains and tasks.

Summary

In this chapter, we explored advanced neural network concepts, including BiLSTM, Attention Mechanisms, Transformer Architecture, GANs for text, and Capsule Networks, each of which holds significance in modern deep learning applications.

Bidirectional Long Short-Term Memory (BiLSTM) was introduced as an extension of LSTM that considers both past and future information in sequence modeling. The architecture's practical implementation was demonstrated in sentiment analysis, highlighting its capability to capture complex patterns in data. The Attention Mechanism was then explained, focusing on its ability to selectively concentrate on relevant parts of the input in Seq2Seq models. This mechanism's practical application was illustrated through language translation examples, showcasing its utility in handling long-range dependencies.

The chapter also delved into Transformer Architecture, a significant advancement that revolutionized NLP. It eliminated recurrence and used attention mechanisms across the entire input sequence, providing parallelization and efficiency. Practical implementation was shown in Named Entity Recognition (NER), with a step-by-step walkthrough of code related to transformer architecture. Generative Adversarial Networks (GANs) for text were introduced, explaining their architecture and working principles. The application of GANs on text datasets was practically demonstrated, emphasizing their role in generating realistic and high-quality text data.

Lastly, Capsule Networks were examined in detail, emphasizing their ability to capture spatial hierarchies and relationships within data. This understanding of spatial relationships sets Capsule Networks apart from traditional CNNs. The chapter explained capsules, dynamic routing, and the architecture of Capsule Networks, including the encoder and decoder phases. Despite challenges such as computational complexity and hyperparameter tuning, Capsule Networks' advantages and applications in various domains such as image recognition, medical imaging, and natural language processing were highlighted.

Overall, this chapter provided a comprehensive understanding of cutting-edge neural network models and mechanisms, integrating theoretical explanations with practical demonstrations. The exploration of these advanced topics has illustrated the diverse and evolving landscape of deep learning, shedding light on innovations that continue to push the boundaries of what machine learning models can achieve.

CHAPTER 9: PRODUCTIONIZING TENSORFLOW MODELS

TensorFlow Models in Production Overview

Taking a TensorFlow model from initial development into full production usage involves bridging the gap between experimental prototyping and real-world deployment. TensorFlow provides an integrated platform to support the full life cycle. In the research phase, TensorFlow enables rapid iteration via Python APIs and experiment tracking through integrations with tools like MLflow and Weights & Biases. Distributed training on GPU clusters accelerates model development. For production deployment, TensorFlow Serving provides a server to optimally serve predictions from trained models. It handles scaling, redundancy, and performance optimization like batching. TensorFlow Serving containers can be deployed on Kubernetes for management.

TensorFlow Extended (TFX) is a production pipeline framework that automates and monitors steps like data preprocessing, model training, evaluation, and deployment. TFX leverages TensorFlow Graphs to track pipeline stages. Once in production, TensorFlow Model Analysis can track key metrics on live models to detect data drift, performance degradation, and outlier behavior over time. This enables fine-tuning models online.

TensorFlow also offers TensorFlow Lite for optimizing models for edge devices, TensorFlow.js for web deployment, and integration with TensorFlow Probability for uncertainty metrics.

Together these provide a comprehensive platform to take models from experimentation to production deployment. But challenges remain around aspects like:

- Monitoring and updating large complex models with millions of parameters.
- Detecting and mitigating biases and ethical issues in models.
- Democratizing production-grade ML development beyond experts.
- Handling concept drift in dynamic real-world data.
- Explaining model behavior and debugging failures.

The TensorFlow team is actively focused on tackling these challenges through advances in model interpretation, robustness, and platform improvements. Initiatives like the TensorFlow Privacy and Responsible AI teams target ethical issues. By providing an end-to-end platform, TensorFlow aims to smooth the transition from research prototype to production system. But real-world complexities continue to pose challenges in deploying, monitoring, and updating models reliably at scale. Further advances on both the algorithmic and systems sides will be key to unlocking the true potential of ML in practice.

TensorFlow Lite

TensorFlow Lite is a deep learning framework developed by Google to deploy machine learning models on mobile and embedded devices. It's a lightweight version of TensorFlow that is designed for low-latency inference, which is especially crucial in resource-constrained environments. TensorFlow Lite's architecture is tailored to meet the challenges of running ML models on devices with limited computational resources, memory, and power.

Architecture and Working

TensorFlow Lite Converter

The TensorFlow Lite Converter plays a central role in converting standard TensorFlow models into a format optimized for on-device execution. The conversion includes quantization, optimizations for size, and various transformations that make the model suitable for mobile and embedded deployment.

- Quantization: It supports techniques like float16 and int8 quantization, which reduces model size and computation resources needed.
- Pruning: Removes unnecessary nodes and parameters from the graph that doesn't contribute to the output, further reducing the size.

TensorFlow Lite Interpreter

The TensorFlow Lite Interpreter is the core component responsible for executing the converted model on the target device.

- Lightweight: It's designed to be minimal and efficient, tailored for mobile and embedded platforms.
- Flexibility: It can run on various platforms, including Android, iOS, and embedded Linux.
- Delegate Mechanism: The delegate mechanism allows the interpreter to offload certain computations to specialized hardware accelerators if available, such as GPU, DSP, or NNAPI on Android devices.

TensorFlow Lite Model File

The TensorFlow Lite model file is a serialized flat buffer file that stores the computational graph and metadata, including weights, biases, and other model parameters.

- Efficient Storage: The format allows for faster load times and efficient execution.
- Compatibility: It supports a subset of TensorFlow operations, optimized for mobile and embedded platforms.

TensorFlow Lite Kernels

Kernels are the implementation of the operations that are used in the model. TensorFlow Lite provides optimized kernels for a wide variety of operations.

- Portable: Written in C++, they are designed to be cross-platform.
- Optimization: The kernels are optimized for size and speed on various platforms, providing efficient execution.

Hardware Acceleration:

TensorFlow Lite supports hardware acceleration through the use of delegates, enabling execution on specialized hardware like Edge TPUs or GPU.

- Delegates: They act as bridges, allowing the TensorFlow Lite interpreter to run operations on the underlying hardware efficiently.
- Extensibility: TensorFlow Lite can be extended to support custom hardware through the delegate interface.

On-Device ML

TensorFlow Lite is designed for on-device machine learning, enabling features like personalization, privacy, and real-time performance.

- Offline Operation: The models can run without internet access.
- Real-time Processing: By being close to the data source and having optimized execution, TensorFlow Lite enables real-time processing of information.

TensorFlow Lite represents a significant step in enabling AI on edge devices. Its architecture is tailored to offer flexibility, efficiency, and ease of deployment across various platforms, balancing the need for computational efficiency with the constraints inherent to mobile and embedded systems. By leveraging quantization, hardware acceleration, and a lightweight interpreter, TensorFlow Lite brings ML models out of data centers and into the hands of users, opening new possibilities for intelligent applications.

TensorFlow Model Production Process

Deploying TensorFlow models into production involves several essential steps to ensure that the model performs well in a real-world environment. Following is a step-by-step walkthrough that provides an insight into this intricate process:

Model Validation and Evaluation

Before deploying, the model should be thoroughly validated and evaluated.

- Validation: Verify that the model is meeting business and technical objectives by using a validation set.
- Evaluation Metrics: Use appropriate metrics like accuracy, precision, recall, F1-score, etc., depending on the problem, to assess the model's performance.

Model Optimization

To ensure that the model performs efficiently in production, optimization steps might be necessary.

- Quantization: Reducing the precision of the model's weights can save memory and computation.

- Pruning: Eliminate unnecessary parameters to make the model smaller and faster.

Converting to TensorFlow Lite

If deploying on mobile or embedded devices, the model can be converted to TensorFlow Lite.

- TensorFlow Lite Converter: This tool transforms TensorFlow models into a format optimized for on-device inference.
- Model Testing: Post conversion, testing on the target devices is crucial to ensure that the model behaves as expected.

Model Versioning

Proper versioning is essential for managing different iterations of the model.

- Version Control: Store different versions of the model and related artifacts, like preprocessing code, in a version-controlled system.
- Documentation: Include detailed documentation for each version regarding changes, performance, etc.

Model Serving with TensorFlow Serving

TensorFlow Serving is a library developed by Google to deploy machine learning models seamlessly.

- Model Containerization: Containerizing the model using tools like Docker ensures that it can run in any environment.
- Configuration: Define the resources, scaling policies, and other configurations needed for serving.
- Deployment: Deploy the containerized model on a server or cloud infrastructure.

Continuous Monitoring and Logging

Once deployed, continuous monitoring is necessary to detect and handle any issues.

- Performance Monitoring: Track the latency, throughput, and other performance metrics.
- Anomaly Detection: Implement systems to detect anomalies in predictions or inputs.
- Logging: Log all predictions, inputs, and other relevant information for debugging and auditing.

Scalability and Load Balancing

Depending on the expected load, the deployment may need to handle a large number of requests.

- Horizontal Scaling: Add more instances of the model to handle increased load.
- Load Balancing: Distribute the incoming requests evenly among the available instances.

A/B Testing and Continuous Improvement

It's essential to keep improving the model by learning from real-world interactions.

- A/B Testing: Compare different versions of the model in production to find the best one.
- Continuous Improvement: Regularly retrain the model with fresh data, implement feedback loops, and deploy improved versions.

Deploying TensorFlow models into production is a complex process involving multiple steps. Careful planning, execution, and continuous monitoring are necessary to ensure that the model operates efficiently, scales according to demand, and evolves as needed. The path from prototype to production involves cross-disciplinary collaboration between data scientists, ML engineers, DevOps, and business teams. A rigorous focus on operational excellence, continuous improvement, and responsible AI practices ultimately determines the real-world impact of TensorFlow models.

TensorFlow Serving - Overview & Architecture

TensorFlow Serving is a flexible, high-performance serving system specifically designed to manage and deploy machine learning models. It's part of the broader TensorFlow ecosystem and is optimized for serving inferences in a production environment. Since we've already discussed some aspects of TensorFlow Serving in the previous section, let us delve deeper into its other essential components and features.

TensorFlow Serving provides a robust, high-performance serving architecture optimized for deploying machine learning models in production environments. It enables taking TensorFlow models trained in Python to scalable, secure serving applications accessed by clients in the real world. Under the hood, TensorFlow Serving is built using several key abstractions and components:

Servables

The core abstraction in TensorFlow Serving. A Servable encapsulates machine learning models, algorithms, and data. It exposes methods for clients to request predictions. For example, a TensorFlow model exported as a SavedModel would be loaded as a TensorFlow Servable.

Loaders

Manage the lifecycle of Servables. Loaders handle loading Servables from storage, serving prediction requests, and unloading them from memory. This simplifies the logic of repeatedly loading and serving evolving models or algorithms.

Sources

Discover new versions of Servables and feed them to Loaders. This decouples model storage from serving layers. Sources can detect updated SavedModels on filesystems or cloud storage like S3.

Managers

Orchestrate the lifecycle of Servables via Loaders and Sources. Managers ensure at most one version of a specific Servable is loaded at a time. The Manager tracks all available Servable versions.

Model Versioning

TensorFlow Serving natively supports serving multiple versions of a model side by side. Clients can request predictions from a specific version to simplify testing and rolling back models. New model versions are loaded from storage via Sources while existing versions serve requests simultaneously.

Monitoring

Integrations with Prometheus, StatsD, and other monitoring systems provide insights into prediction latency, request volumes, model versions in use, hardware utilization and more. This enables tracking model drift.

Batching

For optimized hardware utilization, TensorFlow Serving can intelligently batch multiple prediction requests together before feeding them to models. This amortizes costs like I/O across requests. Batch sizes and delays can be configured to strike an optimal balance.

Scaling

Horizontally scalable by running TensorFlow Serving servers behind load balancers. Kubernetes and Docker Swarm integrations automate scaling up replicas based on load. Supports distributing requests across GPU/TPU accelerators.

APIs

TensorFlow Serving provides performant gRPC endpoints along with a JSON REST API. Client libraries in languages like Python, Java, Go simplify integrating with applications. Streaming APIs support real-time model inferencing on streams of data.

Security

Encrypted communication via TLS and authentication plugins like OAuth2 available. Sensitive model data can be encrypted at rest. Access policies on models can restrict usage.

To sum up my understanding of it, TensorFlow Serving provides a turnkey architecture for taking TensorFlow models and algorithms from development to production deployment with scalability, responsiveness, and reliability. The versatile abstractions enable tailoring the serving architecture to diverse production use cases in areas like computer vision, NLP, recommender systems, and more. Ongoing innovation by Google promises to further optimize TensorFlow Serving for cutting-edge ML deployment paradigms.

Sample Program: Using TensorFlow Serving

Serving models using TensorFlow Serving is a significant step to bring machine learning models into a production environment. Let us go through the practical process of deploying a model using TensorFlow Serving for one of the previously demonstrated examples, such as a sentiment analysis model.

Installation of TensorFlow Serving

First, you need to install TensorFlow Serving. You can do this using Docker, or you can install it directly on your system. Below is how you can pull the TensorFlow Serving Docker image:

```
docker pull tensorflow/serving
```

Exporting Model in Required Format

TensorFlow Serving expects the model in the SavedModel format. If your model is already saved in this format, you're good to go. If not, you'll need to export it:

```
model = load_your_pretrained_model()
model.save("saved_model/my_model")
```

This will create a directory saved_model/my_model, containing the model architecture and weights.

Starting the TensorFlow Serving Docker Container

Start the Docker container with the command below, which mounts the directory containing your saved model and starts the server:

```
docker run -p 8501:8501 --name=tf_model_serving --mount
type=bind,source=$(pwd)/saved_model/my_model,target=/models/my_model -e
MODEL_NAME=my_model -t tensorflow/serving
```

Now TensorFlow Serving is running on port 8501 and serving your model.

Creating Request for Prediction

With the server running, you can now send a request for a prediction. You can create a JSON object representing your input data:

```
import json

data = {
    "signature_name": "serving_default",
    "instances": [{"text_input": "The movie was great!"}]
}
json_data = json.dumps(data)
```

Sending Request to Server

You can now use a library like requests in Python to send the JSON data to the server and receive the prediction:

```
import requests

headers = {"content-type": "application/json"}
url = "http://localhost:8501/v1/models/my_model:predict"
response = requests.post(url, data=json_data, headers=headers)
prediction = response.json()
print(prediction)
```

Handling the Response

The response from the server will include the predicted sentiment, which you can extract and use as needed.

TensorFlow Serving also provides logging and metrics that you can use for monitoring and managing your deployed models. You can integrate it with tools like Prometheus for more advanced monitoring capabilities.

Also, if you need to serve predictions at scale, you can run TensorFlow Serving in a Kubernetes cluster or use other load-balancing solutions. You can also tune various parameters, such as batching configuration, to optimize performance.

This step-by-step walkthrough provides a practical introduction to serving a machine learning model using TensorFlow Serving. By following these steps, you can take a trained model and deploy it in a production-ready environment, accessible via a REST API. Combining TensorFlow Serving with other tools and best practices, you can build a robust, scalable, and efficient solution for serving models to clients.

TensorFlow Serving in Kubernetes Cluster

Deploying TensorFlow Serving within a Kubernetes cluster enhances scalability and reliability. Below are the detailed steps to set up TensorFlow Serving in a Kubernetes environment:

Depending on your requirements and the environment (local, cloud, etc.), you can choose different ways to set up a Kubernetes cluster. For local development, Minikube is a popular choice.

Installing Minikube

Install a Hypervisor

For KVM on Linux, install the kvm2 and qemu-kvm packages using your Linux package manager. eg:

```
sudo apt install kvm2 qemu-kvm
```

Install kubectl

The Kubernetes command-line tool is required to interact with the cluster. Install kubectl using the package manager:

```
sudo apt install kubectl
```

Install Minikube

Download the latest Minikube binary and install it:

```
curl -LO https://storage.googleapis.com/minikube/releases/latest/minikube-linux-amd64
sudo install minikube-linux-amd64 /usr/local/bin/minikube
```

Start Minikube Cluster
Now start your single-node local cluster using:

```
minikube start --vm-driver=kvm2
```

Verify Installation
Check the status of the cluster:

```
minikube status
```

This will install Minikube and start a single-node Kubernetes cluster on your Linux machine that can be used for development and testing workloads.

Creating Deployment for TensorFlow Serving

TensorFlow Serving can be deployed using a Kubernetes Deployment.

Create a YAML File

```
apiVersion: apps/v1
kind: Deployment
metadata:
  name: tf-serving
  labels:
    app: tf-serving
spec:
  replicas: 2
  selector:
    matchLabels:
      app: tf-serving
  template:
    metadata:
      labels:
        app: tf-serving
    spec:
      containers:
```

```yaml
      - name: tf-serving-container
        image: tensorflow/serving
        ports:
        - containerPort: 8501
```

This YAML file describes a Deployment that will run two replicas of the TensorFlow Serving Docker image.

Apply the YAML File

```
kubectl apply -f tf_serving.yaml
```

Exposing TensorFlow Serving

You need to expose the TensorFlow Serving Deployment to make it accessible.

Create a Service

```
kubectl expose deployment tf-serving --type=LoadBalancer --port=8501
```

Get the Service URL

If you are using Minikube, you can get the URL by running:

```
minikube service tf-serving --url
```

Mounting Your Model

You'll need to make your model accessible to TensorFlow Serving within the Kubernetes cluster.

Create a ConfigMap

You can create a Kubernetes ConfigMap to hold your model configuration.

```
kubectl create configmap model-config --from-
file=model_config_file=path/to/your/model.config
```

Update the Deployment to Use the ConfigMap

Modify the tf_serving.yaml to include the ConfigMap as a volume and mount it in the container.

Sending Requests

Now that TensorFlow Serving is accessible, you can send requests to it as you did previously. You can use the URL obtained in step 4 to send your requests.

Monitoring and Scaling

Kubernetes provides built-in tools for monitoring the health and performance of your applications, and you can scale your TensorFlow Serving deployment up or down as needed.

When you're done, you can delete the Kubernetes resources you created.

```
kubectl delete service,deployment tf-serving
minikube stop
```

By following these steps, you can deploy TensorFlow Serving within a Kubernetes cluster, making your machine learning models available in a more scalable and resilient manner. You can further customize and enhance this basic deployment by integrating with other Kubernetes features and third-party tools, depending on your specific needs and requirements. The combination of TensorFlow Serving and Kubernetes offers a powerful solution for deploying, managing, and scaling machine learning models in production environments.

Deploy Text Classification API

Deploying a text classification model as an API allows you to make predictions through HTTP requests, enabling various applications to utilize the model. Let us follow the steps to deploy the previously created text classification model as an API:

Prepare the Model for Serving

Assuming you have the text classification model trained with TensorFlow, you'll want to save it in a format suitable for TensorFlow Serving.

```
model_path = "/path/to/model/directory"
model.save(model_path, save_format="tf")
```

Containerize the Model with Docker

If you want to serve the model inside a container, you'll need to create a Dockerfile.

```
FROM tensorflow/serving
```

```
COPY /path/to/model/directory /models/text_classifier/1
ENV MODEL_NAME text_classifier
```

Build and Run the Docker Image:

```
docker build -t text_classifier .
docker run -p 8501:8501 --name=text_classifier_container text_classifier
```

Set up TensorFlow Serving for Model

If not using Docker, you can directly run TensorFlow Serving to host the model:

```
tensorflow_model_server --port=8501 --model_name=text_classifier --
model_base_path=/path/to/model/directory
```

Creating Flask Application

Flask is a micro web framework for Python that you can use to create the API endpoint.

Install Flask

```
pip install flask
```

Flask Application (app.py)

```
from flask import Flask, request, jsonify
import requests
import json

app = Flask(__name__)

@app.route('/classify', methods=['POST'])
def classify_text():
    content = request.json
    text = content['text']
```

```
    # Preprocess the text as done during training
    processed_text = preprocess(text)  # Implement this function as needed

    # Prepare the request payload
    data = {
        "signature_name": "serving_default",
        "instances": [{"input_text": processed_text}]
    }

    # Send a request to TensorFlow Serving
    response = requests.post('http://localhost:8501/v1/models/text_classifier:predict',
json=data)
    predictions = json.loads(response.text)['predictions']

    # Postprocess the predictions to a readable format
    result = postprocess(predictions)  # Implement this function as needed

    return jsonify(result)

if __name__ == '__main__':
    app.run(port=5000)
```

Deploying the Flask Application

You can deploy the Flask application using a WSGI server like Gunicorn.

Install Gunicorn

```
pip install gunicorn
```

Run the Application with Gunicorn

```
gunicorn -w 4 app:app -b 0.0.0.0:5000
```

Testing the API

You can now test the API by sending a POST request to the endpoint:

```
curl -X POST -H "Content-Type: application/json" -d '{"text":"Sample text for classification"}' http://localhost:5000/classify
```

Scaling and Monitoring

For production use, consider deploying the API on a platform that can scale and monitor the application, such as Kubernetes, as previously discussed.

The above steps can bring a scalable API endpoint for text classification that can be utilized by various applications. It brings together the modeling, preprocessing, serving, and web layers into a cohesive deployment, allowing users to classify text through simple HTTP requests.

Edge Computing

Overview

Edge computing refers to performing computation and data processing closer to the source of data generation rather than relying solely on cloud or remote data centers. It enables low-latency analytics and real-time decision making by situating computation at the "edge" of networks - on devices like smartphones, embedded systems, smart cameras etc.

Key drivers for edge computing include:

- Reducing latency - Critical applications like autonomous vehicles, industrial controls, augmented reality require ultra low latency which edge delivers vs cloud.
- Saving bandwidth - Performing processing locally reduces data transmission costs and network bandwidth usage. Useful in bandwidth constrained environments.
- Improving reliability - Edge applications can continue functioning locally even with temporary loss of connectivity. Critical for systems like healthcare devices, drones etc.
- Enhancing privacy - Sensitive data like user biometrics, industrial data can be processed locally on device without transmitting to the cloud.
- Scaling compute - The exponentially growing number of smart edge devices are an enormous distributed compute resource.

Edge computing complements cloud computing with this distributed processing capability across the continuum from core cloud to devices on the edge. An integrated edge-to-cloud architecture is ideal for many applications.

Use Cases

The given below are some key use cases that benefit from edge computing:

- Autonomous Vehicles - Perform time-sensitive inference like object detection locally using camera data. Helps navigate safely with minimal latency. Cloud supplements with broader learning.

- Industrial IoT - Sensor data from machinery is preprocessed on edge devices before transmitting analytics to the cloud. Enables real-time monitoring and control.

- Augmented Reality - Detect user environment and overlay contextual information instantly using device cameras and sensors. Cloud provides broader world knowledge.

- Smart Homes - On-device speech recognition for virtual assistants allows quick response to user commands. Cloud handles external requests.

- Mobile Apps - Perform key inference like image classification or NLP on-device. Good for privacy. Cloud provides external data.

- Drones - Make flight control decisions using local sensors. Use edge for time-critical maneuvers, cloud for global path planning.

- Healthcare - Wearables monitor patient biometrics locally. Alert caregivers of anomalies in real-time, while transmitting data to cloud for centralized analytics.

TensorFlow Lite for Edge ML

TensorFlow's lightweight edge runtime optimized to serve machine learning models efficiently on edge devices with constraints like lower memory, compute capability and power consumption. It enables deploying ML applications to embedded systems and IoT by supporting execution across a variety of hardware types including mobile phones, Raspberry Pi, through to microcontrollers.

Key capabilities of TensorFlow Lite for edge deployment:

- Cross-Platform Support - TensorFlow Lite runtime can execute on Linux, Windows, Mac as well as microcontrollers like Arm Cortex M series using C/C++ API. Supports mobile platforms including Android and iOS.
- Optimized Inference - Leverages techniques like quantization, pruning, kernel fusion to optimize models and achieve low latency inference. Enables execution within 10s of milliseconds on many devices.
- Lightweight - Significantly smaller runtime footprint compared to full TensorFlow. Makes it usable on memory constrained devices.
- Offline Execution - Does not require constant cloud connectivity. Models can execute

independently using local data. Supplements cloud execution.

- Hardware Acceleration - Takes advantage of special hardware like GPU, DSP, NPU for accelerated inference when available. Falls back to CPU otherwise.
- Model Conversion - Tools to convert TensorFlow models into TensorFlow Lite format out-of-the-box. Allows building in standard TensorFlow then deploying to edge.
- Edge ML Pipeline - Integrated pipeline for optimizing, benchmarking, and deploying models using TensorFlow Lite Converter, evaluation toolkit, runtime etc.

TensorFlow Lite delivers an end-to-end solution for embedding ML inferencing within edge applications spanning from tiny microcontrollers to full-fledged mobile phones and PCs. Combined with core TensorFlow for model development and cloud integration, it enables building an edge-to-cloud system leveraging ML to make intelligent real-time decisions across the continuum from device to data center.

Monitor and Update TensorFlow Models

Model deployment is a critical phase in the machine learning lifecycle, but it is not the end. Continuous monitoring and updating of models are vital to ensure that they perform optimally in a dynamic environment. Following is a detailed look at the processes for updating and monitoring TensorFlow models in production and how they can be applied to one of our previously demonstrated examples.

Updating TensorFlow Models in Production

Updating a model refers to the process of replacing the existing model in production with a newer version. This is often necessary when the underlying data changes, leading to a drift in model performance.

Retraining the Model

Retraining the model on updated data allows it to continue performing well as the underlying patterns in the data evolve.

Steps:

1. Collecting New Data: Collect additional data or updated data reflecting the current state.
2. Preprocessing: Apply the same preprocessing steps used on the original data.
3. Retraining: Train the model using the updated data.
4. Validation: Validate the model to ensure that it meets the required performance metrics.

Version Control

Utilizing version control helps in managing different iterations of the model.

Steps:

1. Create a New Version: Save the newly trained model as a new version.
2. Test: Test the new version alongside the old version to ensure it performs as expected.
3. Deploy: Deploy the new version into production, replacing the old version.

Automated Updating

Automated model updating involves scheduling retraining and deployment to occur automatically at regular intervals or in response to specific triggers.

Steps:

1. Scheduled Retraining: Set up a schedule for regular retraining of the model.
2. Automatic Deployment: Automate the deployment of newly trained models using CI/CD pipelines.

Monitoring TensorFlow Models in Production

Monitoring refers to the ongoing observation of the model's performance and other operational aspects to detect and diagnose issues.

Performance Monitoring

Regularly evaluating the model's predictions to ensure it continues to perform well.

Steps:

1. Collecting Prediction Data: Log the predictions made by the model.
2. Evaluate Metrics: Evaluate performance metrics such as accuracy, precision, and recall.

Operational Monitoring

Observing the technical performance of the model, such as latency, throughput, and resource utilization.

Steps:

1. Monitor Latency: Track how long it takes for the model to make predictions.
2. Monitor Throughput: Observe the number of predictions the model makes per unit of time.
3. Resource Utilization: Monitor the CPU, memory, and network resources utilized by the model.

Anomaly Detection

Detecting unusual patterns that might indicate a problem with the model.

Steps:

1. Set Baselines: Establish normal operating parameters.

2. Detect Anomalies: Use statistical techniques to detect deviations from normal behavior.

Sample Program: Updating and Monitoring Text Classification Model

In the case of our previously demonstrated text classification model, here's how you can practically implement updating and monitoring.

Updating

- Collect Updated Data: Gather new examples of text that reflect current trends.

- Retrain the Model: Use TensorFlow to retrain the model on the new data:

```
model.fit(new_data, epochs=10)
```

- Version Control: Save the new version using TensorFlow's model saving capabilities:

```
model.save('text_classification_model_v2')
```

- Deploy the New Version: Use tools like TensorFlow Serving to deploy the new version.

Monitoring

- Performance Metrics: Regularly evaluate the model's accuracy on a validation dataset.

- Operational Metrics: Utilize logging and monitoring tools to keep an eye on latency and throughput.

- Anomaly Detection: Implement custom logic or use existing monitoring solutions to detect unusual patterns in prediction behavior.

To sum up, the ongoing maintenance of machine learning models in production involves both updating and monitoring. These processes are essential for ensuring that models continue to deliver accurate predictions and operate efficiently in a dynamic environment. By implementing systematic retraining, version control, performance evaluation, and anomaly detection, you can keep your models performing at their best.

Common Errors and Troubleshooting

The deployment and management of TensorFlow models in production come with various challenges and errors, including versioning conflicts, performance degradation, resource utilization, preprocessing discrepancies, latency, and security concerns. Practical solutions to these issues involve a combination of good practices, monitoring, optimization, security measures, and the right use of tools and technologies. Code snippets and scripts tailored to specific errors can aid in implementing these solutions effectively and maintaining the model's efficiency and integrity in a live environment.

Here, I'll detail some common errors and provide practical solutions, along with code snippets, to tackle them.

Model Versioning Conflict

Error

When deploying a new version of the model, conflicts may arise due to improper handling of version numbers or inconsistencies between different versions.

Solution

Implement a systematic version control strategy that maintains a clear record of versions, changes, and compatibility.

Sample Script

```
# Saving a specific version of the model
model.save('model_v1.0')

# Loading a specific version when needed
loaded_model = tf.keras.models.load_model('model_v1.0')
```

Model Performance Degradation

Error

Model performance might degrade over time due to changing patterns in the underlying data (concept drift).

Solution

Monitor model performance regularly and set up a retraining pipeline that adapts to new data patterns.

Sample Script

```
# Regularly evaluate the model
performance_metric = model.evaluate(validation_data)

# If performance drops below a threshold, trigger retraining
if performance_metric < threshold:
    model.fit(new_data)
```

Resource Overutilization

Error

Excessive consumption of CPU, memory, or other resources can hinder the model's performance.

Solution

Monitor resource utilization and consider optimizing the model or using resource management tools.

Sample Script

```
# Example of using Kubernetes to limit resource utilization
apiVersion: v1
kind: ResourceQuota
metadata:
  name: compute-resources
spec:
  limits:
    cpu: '2'
    memory: 2Gi
```

Incompatible Preprocessing

Error

Differences in preprocessing between training and serving can lead to prediction errors.

Solution

Ensure that the same preprocessing steps are applied consistently at both training and prediction time.

Sample Script

```
# Example of using a preprocessing function
def preprocess_input(input_data):
    # Preprocessing steps
    return preprocessed_data

# Apply the same function during both training and prediction
train_data = preprocess_input(raw_train_data)
prediction_input = preprocess_input(raw_prediction_input)
```

Model Serving Latency

Error

High latency during inference can degrade the user experience.

Solution

Monitor latency and consider model optimization techniques or scaling strategies.

Sample Script

```
# Using TensorFlow Model Optimization Toolkit for pruning
import tensorflow_model_optimization as tfmot

prune_low_magnitude = tfmot.sparsity.keras.prune_low_magnitude
pruned_model = prune_low_magnitude(model)

# Update the model with pruning
pruned_model.compile(optimizer='adam',
                loss=tf.keras.losses.SparseCategoricalCrossentropy(from_logits=True),
                metrics=['accuracy'])
```

Model Security Concerns

Error

Unauthorized access or tampering with the deployed model.

Solution

Implement authentication and authorization controls along with encryption, monitoring, and regular audits.

Sample Script

```
# Using Kubernetes RBAC for access control
kind: Role
apiVersion: rbac.authorization.k8s.io/v1
metadata:
  namespace: default
  name: model-reader
rules:
- apiGroups: [""]
  resources: ["models"]
  verbs: ["get", "list"]
```

Summary

In this chapter, we delved into the multifaceted world of deploying and managing machine learning models in production, specifically focusing on TensorFlow. We commenced with an introduction to the challenges and developments in putting ML models into production, followed by an in-depth examination of TensorFlow Lite. We explored its architecture and workings, giving a comprehensive view of how lightweight models can be built for edge devices.

The progression of the chapter then led us into the meticulous process of deploying TensorFlow models after training. TensorFlow Serving became a focal point, shedding light on its essentials and demonstrating practical ways to serve models. The detailed steps to run TensorFlow Serving in a Kubernetes cluster were explained, and we learned how to deploy a text classification API, providing practical insights into real-world applications.

Edge computing and TensorFlow Lite's capability to perform edge computations were also thoroughly examined. The chapter then pivoted to strategies for updating and monitoring TensorFlow models in production, with an emphasis on maintaining efficiency and responding to live changes. Additionally, a comprehensive walkthrough was provided to troubleshoot the most common errors that may arise during deployment, offering practical solutions and relevant scripts for each issue.

Throughout this chapter, the emphasis has been on practical application, ensuring a comprehensive understanding of not only the theoretical aspects but also the hands-on application of these concepts. Whether it's understanding the nuances of TensorFlow Lite, deploying models with Kubernetes, or handling errors in a production environment, the chapter offers a detailed roadmap for anyone looking to navigate the complex landscape of deploying TensorFlow models in production.

Chapter 10: Preparing for TensorFlow Developer Certificate Exam

Revisiting Journey: Learnings So Far

This Chapter serves as a reflection on the extensive learning journey we've embarked on, encapsulating key takeaways from the previous nine chapters that align with the TensorFlow Developer Certificate exam. Following is an overview of what has been covered:

Chapter 1: Introduction to TensorFlow

We began with an introduction to TensorFlow, its history, and its broad applications in machine learning and deep learning. The chapter provided insights into installing TensorFlow, understanding its architecture, and writing simple scripts.

Chapter 2: Deep Learning Basics

The next chapter dived into deep learning fundamentals, exploring neural networks, activation functions, optimizers, loss functions, and other vital concepts. Practical examples were provided to illustrate how deep learning models could be built using TensorFlow.

Chapter 3: Computer Vision and Convolutional Neural Networks

We transitioned into computer vision, learning about Convolutional Neural Networks (CNNs) and their applications in image recognition and classification. Practical demonstrations were given on implementing CNNs for various computer vision tasks using TensorFlow.

Chapter 4: Natural Language Processing and Text Recognition

NLP techniques and text recognition were covered, focusing on processing and cleaning text data. We delved into various models like LSTM, Seq2Seq, and Transformer architecture. Practical demonstrations of tasks like sentiment analysis and named entity recognition provided hands-on experience.

Chapter 5: Model Evaluation and Validation

Model evaluation metrics were discussed in detail, including precision, recall, F1-score, and ROC-AUC. Strategies for data annotation and preparation were thoroughly examined, allowing for practical implementation.

Chapter 6: Regularization Techniques and Addressing Overfitting/Underfitting

We explored overfitting and underfitting, examining techniques to combat these issues, such as regularization, data augmentation, dropout, batch normalization, and early stopping. Practical illustrations helped in understanding the applications of these concepts.

Chapter 7: Advanced Neural Network Aspects

The chapter provided an extensive look into advanced neural network architectures like BiLSTM, Attention Mechanism, Transformer architecture, GANs, and capsule networks. Detailed theoretical insights were accompanied by practical demonstrations, such as using Transformer architecture in NER and applying GANs to text datasets.

Chapter 8: Model Deployment and Production Challenges
The penultimate chapter shed light on the state-of-the-art in deploying ML models, introducing TensorFlow Lite and TensorFlow Serving. We covered everything from serving models to setting up Kubernetes clusters and deploying text classification APIs. Practical steps, error troubleshooting, and strategies for updating and monitoring models in production were provided.

Chapter 9: Edge Computing and Continuous Monitoring
The final chapter elaborated on edge computing, specifically how TensorFlow Lite performs it. We delved into the real-world application of continuous monitoring and model updates, with in-depth explanations and practical demonstrations.

In summary, this learning journey has covered a comprehensive spectrum of topics vital to a TensorFlow developer, starting from basic concepts to advanced neural network architectures, model evaluation, regularization techniques, deployment strategies, edge computing, and continuous monitoring. It's a thorough preparation for the TensorFlow Developer Certificate exam, integrating theoretical understanding with practical application across a wide array of real-world examples. Whether it's building a basic deep learning model or deploying a complex neural network, the chapters have provided the knowledge and skills required to excel in the ever-evolving field of TensorFlow development.

Exam Preparation: Strategies and Tips

As you prepare to take the TensorFlow Developer Certificate exam, maximizing the benefits of the learnings from the previous nine chapters is crucial. Following is a smart eyewalk to the strategies and tips to help you make the best use of the acquired knowledge:

Review and Understand Core Concepts

- Deep Learning Basics: Revisit neural networks, activation functions, optimizers, and loss functions.
- Computer Vision & NLP: Reinforce your understanding of CNNs, LSTM, Seq2Seq, Transformers, and other techniques used in image and text processing.
- Model Evaluation: Ensure a robust grasp of metrics like precision, recall, F1-score, and ROC-AUC.
- Regularization & Overfitting/Underfitting: Understand how to implement regularization techniques, dropout, batch normalization, and early stopping.
- Advanced Architectures: Delve into BiLSTM, attention mechanisms, GANs, and more.
- Model Deployment: Revise TensorFlow Lite, TensorFlow Serving, Kubernetes, edge computing, and continuous monitoring.

Hands-On Practice

- Code Review: Go through the practical examples from each chapter to understand the implementation nuances.
- Build Models: Experiment with creating models using different architectures.
- Deploy Models: Practice deploying models using TensorFlow Serving and setting up a Kubernetes cluster.
- Troubleshoot Errors: Revisit the solutions provided for potential errors and understand the underlying logic.

Utilize Additional Resources

- Official TensorFlow Documentation: Review the official documentation for up-to-date information and best practices.
- Online Tutorials & Courses: Engage with reputable online platforms that offer specialized TensorFlow tutorials and courses.
- Community Engagement: Participate in forums and communities dedicated to TensorFlow. Engaging with peers can provide different perspectives and solutions to problems.

Focus on Time Management

- Set a Study Schedule: Plan a detailed study schedule to allocate time to review each chapter and practice exercises.
- Simulate Exam Conditions: Try taking practice tests under exam-like conditions to gauge your readiness and comfort with the time constraints.

Analyze Your Strengths and Weaknesses

- Self-Assessment: Identify areas where you excel and areas that need improvement. Focus on reinforcing the weak spots.
- Seek Peer Review: If possible, have someone knowledgeable review your work to provide constructive feedback.

Maintain a Healthy Study Routine

- Take Breaks: Regular breaks can enhance focus and efficiency.
- Stay Healthy: Ensure proper sleep, diet, and exercise. Physical well-being plays a significant role in mental performance.

Stay Updated

Follow Industry Trends: Keep abreast of the latest trends and updates in TensorFlow and machine learning.

Adopt a Holistic Approach

Combine Theory with Practical Application: The chapters have provided a blend of theoretical understanding and practical application. Ensure that you can apply theoretical concepts practically.

Develop a Growth Mindset

- Embrace Challenges: Recognize that challenges are opportunities for growth.
- Learn from Mistakes: Mistakes are valuable learning experiences. Reflect on them and understand what can be done differently.

The journey towards the TensorFlow Developer Certificate exam is an integrated process that requires understanding core concepts, practical application, effective time management, continual learning, and maintaining a healthy routine. Leveraging these strategies and aligning them with your learning style will enable you to make the most out of the rich content covered in the previous chapters, setting the stage for a successful examination experience.

Hands-on Labs and Coding: Challenges

Following are a few coding challenges around TensorFlow and working with ML models, covering various aspects of what you've learned. I'll provide a detailed description of the case scenarios and hints to walkthrough you through solving them.

Challenge 1: Image Classification with CNN

Create a Convolutional Neural Network (CNN) to classify images from the CIFAR-10 dataset. Your task is to build a model that achieves at least 85% accuracy on the validation set.

Hints

Preprocess the data by normalizing and augmenting images.
Consider using layers like Conv2D, MaxPooling2D, Dropout, and Dense.
Experiment with different activation functions and optimizers.

Challenge 2: Sentiment Analysis using LSTM

Develop an LSTM-based model to perform sentiment analysis on a given text dataset. You need to preprocess the text data, create word embeddings, and build a model that can classify the sentiments as positive or negative.

Hints

Tokenize the text and convert it to sequences.
Use an Embedding layer for word embeddings.
Experiment with Bidirectional LSTM layers.

Challenge 3: Time Series Prediction with RNN

You have been given a time series dataset representing sales of a product. You need to create a Recurrent Neural Network (RNN) that can forecast future sales.

Hints

Normalize the data and create sequences for time series analysis.
Consider using layers like LSTM or GRU for sequential patterns.
Pay attention to the loss function suitable for regression tasks.

Challenge 4: Text Generation using GAN

Build a Generative Adversarial Network (GAN) that can generate realistic textual content based on a given corpus. You will need to define both generator and discriminator networks.

Hints

Represent the text using appropriate embeddings or encodings.
Use dense layers with appropriate activation functions for generator and discriminator.
Experiment with training techniques specific to GANs.

Challenge 5: Model Deployment with TensorFlow Serving

Deploy a previously trained TensorFlow model using TensorFlow Serving. Create a client that can send requests to the server, process responses, and handle different types of data input.

Hints

Utilize TensorFlow's SavedModel format.
Configure TensorFlow Serving with Docker or in a Kubernetes cluster.
Implement a client using gRPC or REST API.

Challenge 6: Fine-Tuning Transformer for Named Entity Recognition

You are tasked with fine-tuning a pre-trained Transformer model like BERT for Named Entity Recognition (NER) on a specific dataset.

Hints

Use the transformers library to load the pre-trained model.
Create appropriate tokenization and data preprocessing for the task.
Define a suitable loss function and training strategy for fine-tuning.

Challenge 7: Object Detection with Custom Dataset

Build an object detection model to identify specific objects within images using a custom dataset. You'll need to annotate the data, preprocess it, and create a model to detect the objects.

Hints

Consider using pre-trained models and fine-tuning.
Pay attention to the annotation and data preprocessing.
Experiment with different architectures like SSD or Faster R-CNN.

Challenge 8: Text Summarization using Seq2Seq

Implement a text summarization model using sequence-to-sequence architecture. The goal is to take a large text document and generate a concise summary.

Hints

Utilize encoder-decoder architecture with attention mechanism.
Preprocess the text into appropriate input and target sequences.
Experiment with different sequence lengths and tokenization methods.

Challenge 9: Reinforcement Learning for Game Playing

Develop a reinforcement learning agent that can play and win a particular game (e.g., Tic Tac Toe or Flappy Bird). Define the environment, rewards, and train the agent.

Hints

Define the state, action, reward, and transition logic.
Consider algorithms like Q-learning or deep Q-networks (DQN).
Experiment with different reward functions and training strategies.

Challenge 10: Anomaly Detection in Time Series Data

You have a time series dataset representing the metrics of a server. Your task is to create a model that can detect unusual patterns or anomalies in the data.

Hints

Explore statistical methods or autoencoder architecture.

Consider using sliding windows for sequential data.
Tune the threshold for anomaly detection carefully.

Challenge 11: Style Transfer for Text

Implement a style transfer model that can rewrite a given text in a different tone or style (e.g., formal to informal).

Hints

Consider using seq2seq models with attention or transformer-based architectures.
Experiment with different loss functions to capture style and content.
Preprocess the data to represent different styles effectively.

Challenge 12: Multimodal Learning for Image and Text

Build a model that can learn from both image and text data. An example task might be to predict the sentiment of a product review, considering both the review text and an associated image.

Hints

Preprocess both text and image data.
Consider using CNN for image processing and RNN/LSTM for text.
Explore methods to combine or fuse these modalities within the model.

Challenge 13: Deploying Edge AI with TensorFlow Lite

Deploy a machine learning model on an edge device (like a smartphone or IoT device) using TensorFlow Lite. Optimize the model for performance and size constraints.

Hints

Experiment with model quantization and pruning.
Consider the specific constraints of the target device.
Test the deployment in a real or emulated environment.

Challenge 14: Creating a Recommendation System

Build a recommendation system for a retail website using collaborative filtering or content-based methods.

Hints

Explore different recommendation algorithms like matrix factorization or neural collaborative filtering.
Preprocess the data to represent user-item interactions.

Experiment with personalization and scalability aspects.

Challenge 15: Generative Adversarial Network (GAN) for Image Synthesis

Develop a GAN to generate new images of faces that don't exist in real life. You'll need to design both the generator and discriminator networks.

Hints

Experiment with different architectures like DCGAN.
Consider using a pre-trained model for feature extraction.
Pay attention to training stability and convergence.

Challenge 16: Neural Style Transfer for Art Creation

Implement a neural style transfer algorithm to combine the content of one image with the style of another. Think of creating new artwork by merging the styles of famous painters with your photographs.

Hints

Explore existing research and implementations for guidance.
Work on loss functions that balance content and style.
Experiment with different layers and weights for style representation.

Challenge 17: Natural Language Understanding with Transformers

Build a model to understand and respond to natural language queries, like a virtual assistant. Utilize transformer architecture for this purpose.

Hints

Consider using pre-trained models like BERT or GPT.
Fine-tune the model on a specific task like question answering or command processing.
Experiment with different tokenization and input formats.

Challenge 18: Multi-task Learning with Shared Representations

Develop a model that can perform multiple tasks simultaneously (e.g., object detection, classification, and segmentation) with shared representations.

Hints

Design a shared backbone with task-specific heads.
Carefully manage the loss functions and training strategy.
Consider using multitask learning frameworks and methodologies.

Challenge 19: Reinforcement Learning in Simulated Environment

Train a reinforcement learning agent to navigate through a simulated environment (e.g., maze-solving or robotic control).

Hints

Utilize existing simulation environments like OpenAI Gym.
Experiment with different RL algorithms and policies.
Focus on reward shaping and environment interactions.

Challenge 20: Graph Neural Networks for Social Analysis

Implement a graph neural network to analyze social network data. You may choose a task like community detection, link prediction, or user profiling.

Hints

Explore graph convolutional networks (GCNs) or GraphSAGE.
Preprocess the graph data and consider node and edge features.
Experiment with different aggregation and pooling methods.

Challenge 21: Fairness and Bias Analysis in Models

Conduct an analysis of fairness and bias in a machine learning model. Identify potential biases in the data and model and suggest mitigation strategies.

Hints

Utilize fairness metrics and bias detection tools.
Experiment with different preprocessing and in-processing techniques.
Consider the ethical implications and potential impacts.

Challenge 22: End-to-End Speech Recognition System

Build an end-to-end speech recognition system that converts spoken language into written text.

Hints

Experiment with architectures like RNNs, LSTMs, or transformer-based models.
Focus on audio preprocessing, feature extraction, and alignment.
Consider using existing datasets and benchmarks for evaluation.

Challenge 23: Adaptive Learning Rates for Optimizing Models

Experiment with adaptive learning rates and optimization strategies to improve model convergence and training speed.

Hints

Explore methods like Adam, RMSProp, and learning rate schedules.
Conduct systematic experiments to understand the impact.
Consider using visualizations to analyze convergence patterns.

Challenge 24: Transfer Learning for Low-resource Languages

Apply transfer learning techniques to create models for low-resource languages or tasks, such as sentiment analysis or translation for a language with limited data.

Hints

Utilize pre-trained models and fine-tuning strategies.
Experiment with data augmentation and synthetic data generation.
Consider the cultural and linguistic aspects of the target language.

Challenge 25: Anomaly Detection in Time-Series Data

Implement an anomaly detection system for time-series data, such as detecting fraud in financial transactions or equipment failure in an industrial setting.

Hints

Experiment with LSTM, autoencoders, or statistical methods.
Focus on feature engineering, like seasonal decomposition or Fourier transforms.
Test the model with different types of anomalies and noise.

Challenge 26: Multi-modal Learning for Healthcare

Develop a multi-modal learning system that takes both medical images and structured data (e.g., patient records) to predict a health outcome.

Hints

Consider different fusion techniques for image and tabular data.

Focus on interpretability and ethical considerations.
Collaborate with healthcare experts for domain knowledge.

Challenge 27: Human-in-the-loop Machine Learning

Design a human-in-the-loop system where human experts can interact, correct, and guide the machine learning model's decisions, like in document classification or medical diagnosis.

Hints

Implement interfaces for user interaction and feedback.
Experiment with active learning and uncertainty estimation.
Evaluate the system's effectiveness with real users.

Challenge 28: Large-Scale Graph Analytics

Perform large-scale graph analytics on a massive social network or web graph, targeting problems like community detection, influence propagation, or personalized recommendations.

Hints

Utilize distributed computing frameworks like Apache Spark.
Experiment with scalable graph algorithms and representations.
Consider efficiency and scalability challenges.

Challenge 29: Personalized Recommendation System

Build a personalized recommendation system that learns from user behavior and provides tailored suggestions, like in e-commerce or media streaming platforms.

Hints

Implement collaborative filtering, matrix factorization, or deep learning techniques.
Focus on personalization, diversity, and real-time adaptability.
Consider multi-objective optimization for business and user goals.

Challenge 30: Quantum Machine Learning Algorithms

Explore the intersection of quantum computing and machine learning by implementing a quantum machine learning algorithm.

Hints

Consider using quantum libraries like Qiskit or Cirq.
Focus on understanding quantum principles and algorithms.
Experiment with hybrid classical-quantum models.

Summary

Finally, this chapter encompassed a comprehensive review of the entire course, delving into the essential components necessary for the TensorFlow Developer Certificate Exam. The chapter began with a robust conclusion of all nine preceding chapters, summarizing key aspects from foundational TensorFlow syntax to advanced techniques such as GANs, Transformers, and deploying models into production.

The second section offered strategic insights, presenting detailed guidance on how to leverage the accumulated knowledge effectively. This portion focused on maximizing understanding, revision strategies, practice methods, and practical tips to ensure readiness for the exam, promoting an integrated approach to learning and implementation.

Next, the chapter provided an engaging series of coding challenges. These challenges ranged across various complexities and covered diverse applications like anomaly detection, human-in-the-loop machine learning, quantum algorithms, and federated learning. The scenarios were meticulously crafted to encourage creative problem-solving and a hands-on approach to TensorFlow and machine learning models.

The final section maintained the momentum with an assortment of surprise challenges, each escalating in complexity and probing deeper into cutting-edge areas of machine learning and TensorFlow. These final challenges not only provided a stimulating examination of the course's content but also inspired innovative thinking and exploration into novel, exciting realms of technology. Together, these elements fused to create a rich and multifaceted conclusion to the course, highlighting the breadth and depth of the content while simultaneously paving the way for future exploration and growth.

Thank You

Index

A

B

C

D

E

F

G

I

K

L

M

N

O

P

R

S

T

U

V

W

Epilogue

As we approach the final pages of this all-encompassing exploration into TensorFlow and Machine Learning, we find ourselves thinking back on a journey that was packed with moments of discovery and innovation as well as struggles and victories. What started out as an overview of the fundamental concepts has evolved into a comprehensive knowledge of a subject area that continues to test the limits of what is considered feasible.

You have been led through the complex terrain of machine learning through the chapters of this book, which you have been reading. They have been instructed on how to construct, optimize, and deploy models that are able to identify patterns, make predictions, and even generate new creations for themselves. From the most fundamental aspects of data processing and model training to the most advanced realms of Bidirectional LSTM, attention mechanisms, and Generative Adversarial Networks, the purpose of this guide has been to demystify complex concepts in order to make them more approachable and applicable. However, more than just a collection of instructions and examples, this book has been a wealth of information. This serves as a powerful illustration of the transformative potential of machine learning as well as the boundless opportunities that it provides. It has been demonstrated that these technologies are not limited to the realms of science fiction; rather, they are instruments that we can employ to solve problems that exist in the real world, improve lives, and propel innovation.

The book has a practical orientation, and it places a strong emphasis on learning through hands-on experience. The authors' goal was to bridge the gap between theory and application with this book. You are not only taught the "how," but also the "why," ensuring that the knowledge gained is grounded in understanding and is capable of being applied across a wide variety of domains and challenges. The path towards deploying models into production, which is frequently considered to be a daunting transition, has been illuminated. This has provided insights into the tools, techniques, and best practices that ensure a seamless transition from development to deployment. This emphasis on real-world application adds value beyond measure in a context in which the capability of putting models into action is just as important as developing them in the first place.

Those individuals who are looking to validate their skills and gain recognition in the professional sphere now have a clear and focused pathway to follow as a result of the alignment of the book with the TensorFlow Developer Certificate exam. This book has made every effort to provide you with the information, capabilities, and self-assurance necessary to achieve your goals by adhering to the goals and standards established by the certification. The realization that learning in the field of machine learning and TensorFlow is an ongoing process has been perhaps the most eye-opening and life-changing experience that has come out of this journey. Because new scientific discoveries and technological advancements are constantly being made, there is always going to be more that needs to be discovered, understood, and invented. The conclusion of this book does not mark the end of our educational journey; rather, it is a landmark, a chance to take stock of how far we've come and to look ahead to exciting new experiences that lie ahead of us.

In conclusion, the purpose of this book was to serve as more than just a manual; rather, it was intended to be a friend, a teacher, and a motivational tool. You are not only encouraged to learn from it, but also to think, innovate, and contribute to it. Every reader is a trailblazer and an explorer in the ever-expanding world of machine learning, and they each have the ability to influence what the future holds. I wish that reading this book will serve as a stepping stone towards a future rich in exploration, creativity, and making a difference for the better. The journey up to this point has been fruitful and gratifying, and the road that lies ahead is replete with opportunities. Continue to learn new things, discover new things, and create new things. You are about to enter the world of TensorFlow, where the opportunities are virtually limitless.

www.ingramcontent.com/pod-product-compliance
Lightning Source LLC
Chambersburg PA
CBHW080212170726
48282CB00030B/1091
9788119177325